Immigration to North America

South American Immigrants

Larry McCaffrey

D1539968

Immigration to North America

South American Immigrants

Larry McCaffrey

Senior Consulting Editor Stuart Anderson
former Associate Commissioner for Policy and Planning,
US. Citizenship and Immigration Services

Mason Crest
450 Parkway Drive, Suite D
Broomall, PA 19008
www.masoncrest.com

©2017 by Mason Crest, an imprint of National Highlights, Inc.

Printed and bound in the United States of America.

CPSIA Compliance Information: Batch #INA2016.
For further information, contact Mason Crest at 1-866-MCP-Book.

First printing
1 3 5 7 9 8 6 4 2

Library of Congress Cataloging-in-Publication Data

on file at the Library of Congress
ISBN: 978-1-4222-3690-1 (hc)
ISBN: 978-1-4222-8107-9 (ebook)

Immigration to North America series ISBN: 978-1-4222-3679-6

Table of Contents

KEY ICONS TO LOOK FOR:

 Words to Understand: These words with their easy-to-understand definitions will increase the reader's understanding of the text, while building vocabulary skills.

 Sidebars: This boxed material within the main text allows readers to build knowledge, gain insights, explore possibilities, and broaden their perspectives by weaving together additional information to provide realistic and holistic perspectives.

 Research Projects: Readers are pointed toward areas of further inquiry connected to each chapter. Suggestions are provided for projects that encourage deeper research and analysis.

 Text-Dependent Questions: These questions send the reader back to the text for more careful attention to the evidence presented there.

 Series Glossary of Key Terms: This back-of-the book glossary contains terminology used throughout this series. Words found here increase the reader's ability to read and comprehend higher-level books and articles in this field.

The Changing Face of the United States

Marian L. Smith, Historian
U.S. Citizenship and Immigration Services

Americans commonly assume that immigration today is very different than immigration of the past. The immigrants themselves appear to be unlike immigrants of earlier eras. Their language, their dress, their food, and their ways seem strange. At times people fear too many of these new immigrants will destroy the America they know. But has anything really changed? Do new immigrants have any different effect on America than old immigrants a century ago? Is the American fear of too much immigration a new development? Do immigrants really change America more than America changes the immigrants? The very subject of immigration raises many questions.

In the United States, immigration is more than a chapter in a history book. It is a continuous thread that links the present moment to the first settlers on North American shores. From the first colonists' arrival until today, immigrants have been met by Americans who both welcomed and feared them. Immigrant contributions were always welcome—on the farm, in the fields, and in the factories. Welcoming the poor, the persecuted, and the "huddled masses" became an American principle. Beginning with the original Pilgrims' flight from religious persecution in the 1600s, through the Irish migration to escape starvation in the 1800s, to the relocation of Central Americans seeking refuge from civil wars in the 1980s and 1990s, the United States has considered itself a haven for the destitute and the oppressed.

But there was also concern that immigrants would not adopt American ways, habits, or language. Too many immigrants might overwhelm America. If so, the dream of the Founding Fathers for United States government and society would be destroyed. For this reason, throughout American history some have argued that limiting or ending immigration is our patriotic duty. Benjamin Franklin feared there were so many German immigrants in Pennsylvania the Colonial Legislature would begin speaking German. "Progressive" leaders of the early 1900s feared that immigrants who could not read and understand the English language were not only exploited by "big business," but also served as the foundation for "machine politics" that undermined the U.S. Constitution. This theme continues today, usually voiced by those who bear no malice toward immigrants but who want to preserve American ideals.

Have immigrants changed? In colonial days, when most colonists were of English descent, they considered Germans, Swiss, and French immigrants as different. They were not "one of us" because they spoke a different language. Generations later, Americans of German or French descent viewed Polish, Italian, and Russian immigrants as strange. They were not "like us" because they had a different religion, or because they did not come from a tradition of constitutional government. Recently, Americans of Polish or Italian descent have seen Nicaraguan, Pakistani, or Vietnamese immigrants as too different to be included. It has long been said of American immigration that the latest ones to arrive usually want to close the door behind them.

It is important to remember that fear of individual immigrant groups seldom lasted, and always lessened. Benjamin Franklin's anxiety over German immigrants disappeared after those immigrants' sons and daughters helped the nation gain independence in the Revolutionary War. The Irish of the mid-1800s were among the most hated immigrants, but today we all wear green on St. Patrick's Day. While a century ago it was feared that Italian and other Catholic immigrants would vote as directed by the Pope, today that controversy is only a vague memory. Unfortunately, some ethnic groups continue their efforts to earn acceptance. The African

Americans' struggle continues, and some Asian Americans, whose families have been in America for generations, are the victims of current anti-immigrant sentiment.

Time changes both immigrants and America. Each wave of new immigrants, with their strange language and habits, eventually grows old and passes away. Their American-born children speak English. The immigrants' grandchildren are completely American. The strange foods of their ancestors—spaghetti, baklava, hummus, or tofu—become common in any American restaurant or grocery store. Much of what the immigrants brought to these shores is lost, principally their language. And what is gained becomes as American as St. Patrick's Day, Hanukkah, or Cinco de Mayo, and we forget that it was once something foreign.

Recent immigrants are all around us. They come from every corner of the earth to join in the American Dream. They will continue to help make the American Dream a reality, just as all the immigrants who came before them have done.

Welcome to the
United States
A Guide for New
Immigrants

UNITED STATES OF AMERICA Department of Homeland Security

PERMANENT RESIDENT CARD

UNITED STATES OF AMER

We recommend you use this enve...

protect your new card.

The Changing Face of Canada

Peter A. Hammerschmidt
former First Secretary, Permanent Mission of Canada to the United Nations

Throughout Canada's history, immigration has shaped and defined the very character of Canadian society. The migration of peoples from every part of the world into Canada has profoundly changed the way we look, speak, eat, and live. Through close and distant relatives who left their lands in search of a better life, all Canadians have links to immigrant pasts. We are a nation built by and of immigrants.

Two parallel forces have shaped the history of Canadian immigration. The enormous diversity of Canada's immigrant population is the most obvious. In the beginning came the enterprising settlers of the "New World," the French and English colonists. Soon after came the Scottish, Irish, and Northern and Central European farmers of the 1700s and 1800s. As the country expanded westward during the mid-1800s, migrant workers began arriving from China, Japan, and other Asian countries. And the turbulent twentieth century brought an even greater variety of immigrants to Canada, from the Caribbean, Africa, India, and Southeast Asia.

So while English- and French-Canadians are the largest ethnic groups in the country today, neither group alone represents a majority of the population. A large and vibrant multicultural mix makes up the rest, particularly in Canada's major cities. Toronto, Vancouver, and Montreal alone are home to people from over 200 ethnic groups!

Less obvious but equally important in the evolution of Canadian immigration has been hope. The promise of a better life lured Europeans and

Americans seeking cheap (sometimes even free) farmland. Thousands of Scots and Irish arrived to escape grinding poverty and starvation. Others came for freedom, to escape religious and political persecution. Canada has long been a haven to the world's dispossessed and disenfranchised— Dutch and German farmers cast out for their religious beliefs, black slaves fleeing the United States, and political refugees of despotic regimes in Europe, Africa, Asia, and South America.

The two forces of diversity and hope, so central to Canada's past, also shaped the modern era of Canadian immigration. Following the Second World War, Canada drew heavily on these influences to forge trailblazing immigration initiatives.

The catalyst for change was the adoption of the Canadian Bill of Rights in 1960. Recognizing its growing diversity and Canadians' changing attitudes towards racism, the government passed a federal statute barring discrimination on the grounds of race, national origin, color, religion, or sex. Effectively rejecting the discriminatory elements in Canadian immigration policy, the Bill of Rights forced the introduction of a new policy in 1962. The focus of immigration abruptly switched from national origin to the individual's potential contribution to Canadian society. The door to Canada was now open to every corner of the world.

Welcoming those seeking new hopes in a new land has also been a feature of Canadian immigration in the modern era. The focus on economic immigration has increased along with Canada's steadily growing economy, but political immigration has also been encouraged. Since 1945, Canada has admitted tens of thousands of displaced persons, including Jewish Holocaust survivors, victims of Soviet crackdowns in Hungary and Czechoslovakia, and refugees from political upheaval in Uganda, Chile, and Vietnam.

Prior to 1978, however, these political refugees were admitted as an exception to normal immigration procedures. That year, Canada revamped its refugee policy with a new Immigration Act that explicitly affirmed Canada's commitment to the resettlement of refugees from oppression. Today, the admission of refugees remains a central part of

Canadian immigration law and regulations.

Amendments to economic and political immigration policy have continued, refining further the bold steps taken during the modern era. Together, these initiatives have turned Canada into one of the world's few truly multicultural states.

Unlike the process of assimilation into a "melting pot" of cultures, immigrants to Canada are more likely to retain their cultural identity, beliefs, and practices. This is the source of some of Canada's greatest strengths as a society. And as a truly multicultural nation, diversity is not seen as a threat to Canadian identity. Quite the contrary—diversity is Canadian identity.

1 SOUTH AMERICANS: THE OTHER LATINOS

There's no doubt Latin America is making a mark on the culture of the United States and Canada—from pop music stars like Shakira to the rhythms of the cumbia and the cha-cha-cha in elegant nightclubs, from the spicy taste of salsa (more popular in the United States now than ketchup) to the smattering of Spanish words and phrases that have found their way into the English language.

In ways large and small, Hispanics are changing the face of North America. By January 2003, they had officially surpassed African Americans as the largest minority group in the United States; about one in every eight U.S. residents now claims Hispanic heritage. Puerto Rican journalist Juan González refers to "the Latinization of the United States." His point is well taken: the country has, in fact, become the world's fifth-largest Hispanic nation. Canada, meanwhile, does not claim quite so large a Hispanic population. Still, of the approximately 36 million Canadians counted in the country's 2011 census, nearly 400,000—more than 1 percent of the total population—were born in Mexico, Central America, or South America. Clearly, Latinos are in North America to stay.

Not surprisingly, when the Hispanic community in North

◀ Since the 1960s, the number of South American immigrants to the United States has increased dramatically. Today the South American community in the U.S. is more than 3 million people, and approximately 80,000 new immigrants join them each year.

America is written about or discussed, the focus is often on the cultural groups whose homelands are closest to the United States and who, partly for this reason, tend to have the largest U.S. populations. These groups include Mexicans, Central Americans, and Caribbean islanders such as Cubans and Puerto Ricans.

But there's a whole other story—many stories, in fact— buried beneath the more familiar surface of the Latino experience. It's a story rich with the colors and flavors of another America, a land whose breathtaking range of cultures is matched only by the stunning variety of its topography—from snow-capped Andean peaks to warm Caribbean beaches, from the world's driest desert to its largest rain forest, from the remote, windswept pampas to the bustling steel-and-concrete modernity of metropolises like Buenos Aires, Rio de Janeiro, and Caracas. It's the story of people whose journey to the United States or Canada began in South America.

South Americans may be in the United States in smaller numbers than Mexicans, Central Americans, or Caribbean islanders, but their presence is strong and growing. Many have chosen to make North America, with the abundance of freedoms and opportunities it offers, their permanent home. They have become proud "Americans," in the limited sense of that word— although many will say they have always been Americans, since America for them is not just the United States, but rather one enormous land that stretches from above the Arctic Circle in Canada to the Tierra del Fuego in southernmost Argentina.

 Words to Understand in This Chapter

pampas—extensive, treeless plains in South America.

privatization—the selling of government-owned enterprises to private corporations (for example, oil companies, water and electrical utilities).

South American immigrants play soccer in a rec league in Newport, Rhode Island.

Diverse Peoples

For those lucky enough to meet a Colombian, or a Brazilian, or a Chilean, it wouldn't be a good idea to ask for his or her favorite taco recipe. The cuisine of South America is as different from Mexican food as an Italian fettuccine is from a German bratwurst. It also differs from country to country, and even, in many cases, from region to region within a single South American country.

But then, much about South America's peoples differs from country to country. In fact, there's very little one can point to as a common characteristic of South Americans. It can't even be said that they all speak Spanish: Brazil, by far the largest country of South America, was colonized by Portugal, and so Brazilians speak Portuguese. Many indigenous people speak one of hundreds of native languages and dialects—for example, many Andean people still speak the Quechua or Aymara of their ancestors. And Guyana, another South American nation that sends many immigrants to North America, is an English-speaking country. Dutch is the official language of Suriname.

One also can't make assumptions about the income or educational level of South Americans living in North America (not that this is a good idea with any cultural group). Some are quite wealthy, well traveled, and highly educated; they might seem, to a casual observer, more European than Latin American. Some come to the United States or Canada to study, travel, or do business. But others come to North America out of desperation, fleeing the horrors of war or of grinding poverty. After their arrival, these different groups are likely to continue to experience dramatically dissimilar circumstances.

Overall, South Americans in the United States (and Canada) are more likely to have a higher education and income level than Mexicans, Central Americans, or Caribbean islanders. That difference can probably be attributed to South America's greater distance. It's more conceivable for a poor Mexican or Salvadoran to gather all his family's resources and make the journey to *El Norte* to create a new life than it is for a poor Quechua in the mountains of Peru. It's also true that some South American countries, like Argentina and Uruguay, are generally wealthier and more able to offer a better education to their citizens.

Why They Emigrate

Little has been written about South American immigrants as a group. Part of the reason is that large-scale immigration from South to North America has been a relatively recent trend. The U.S. Immigration and Naturalization Service (INS) recorded just 19,662 South American immigrants during the decade 1940–1949. The following decade, the numbers rose significantly, to 78,418, but that still represented fewer than 8,000 newcomers per year. The period 1960–1969 saw 250,754 South American immigrants admitted into the United States, and the numbers continued to rise dramatically over the final three decades of the 20th century, standing at more than 570,000 in 1990–1999, and at more than 850,000 in 2000–2009.

It's impossible to reduce a phenomenon as complex as immigration to a few simple factors; a multitude of circumstances may influence an individual's decision to leave the land of his or her birth to start a new life in another country. Broadly, however, immigration trends are affected by political and economic conditions. There is little incentive for large groups of people to go to a country that has an oppressive government and scant economic opportunities; by the same token, there is little incentive to leave a country that is prosperous, socially harmonious, politically free, and at peace—particularly when the destination is a distant nation with an unfamiliar language and culture. But when poverty at home is widespread, or when violence and repression abound, many people will be willing to gamble on finding a better life elsewhere.

Much of the recent increase in immigration to North America from South America can be understood in these terms. Clearly, North America has many attractions for potential immigrants, including abundant freedoms and economic opportunities. But many South American nations over the last decades have been beset by serious political and economic problems, including repressive military dictatorships, bloody insurgencies, and a severe debt crisis that rocked the region at the end of the 1980s and that continues to reverberate today.

The United States and South America

Critics of U.S. foreign policy say that the United States has not been blameless in Latin America's economic and political problems. Rather than promoting human rights and social justice, these critics charge, the United States in the past frequently supported corrupt Latin American regimes—even brutal dictators—in order to protect its own economic and strategic interests in the region. In a few instances the United States helped overthrow democratically elected governments, with disastrous consequences for the people of the countries in question.

U.S. policy toward Latin America during the second half of the 20th century must be understood against the backdrop of the Cold War—a struggle for global political supremacy between the United States and the Soviet Union. The two countries, which had been uneasy allies in the fight against Nazi Germany during World War II, became bitter rivals in the postwar period. In their efforts to win strategic advantage and thwart the ambitions of the other side, both the United States and the Soviet Union attempted to enlist the support of other nations. For the United States, preventing the Soviet Union from gaining a foothold in the Western Hemisphere was of paramount importance. Thus American policymakers were willing to support even the most repressive and corrupt Latin American regimes as long as they were anti-communist.

In the 1960s and beyond, the U.S. commitment to democratic and social reforms in Latin America was at best tepid. U.S. officials had a tendency to view liberal or socialist Latin American politicians as potential allies of the Soviet Union and thus to undermine them. That is one reason why the South America of the 1970s and 1980s was dominated by dictators.

Although the Cold War ended with the collapse of the Soviet Union in 1991, U.S. policy, in the opinion of some critics, continues to stand in the way of social progress in Latin America. In recent years the United States has promoted an economic model that emphasizes the opening up of markets and the *privatization* of government-run enterprises in Latin America and elsewhere. In some South American countries, at least in the short run, unemployment and poverty have risen sharply.

If U.S. policies have contributed to problems in South America, many South American intellectuals are increasingly looking at their own leaders, institutions, and policies as the primary culprits for their countries' troubles. To these analysts the fault for poorly functioning economies, for example, lies primarily with the politicians who have protected an inefficient and bloated public sector, blocked foreign investment, and prevented the establishment of a stable currency that is free from political manipulation.

This book will provide an overview of immigration from all of South America, giving special attention to the countries that have contributed the greatest number of immigrants to North America. By tracing a bit of the recent history of those countries, and by examining the experiences of their people who have immigrated to the United States and Canada, we can begin to get a glimpse into the story of the South Americans and how they have changed the face of North America.

 Text-Dependent Questions

1. What percentage of Canadians are Hispanic?

2. What are some reasons why South Americans leave their home countries and migrate to the United States or Canada?

 Research Project

Using a library or the Internet, research one of South America's countries. In a box, present the following basic information: Total area; Highest point; Lowest point; Population; Capital city; Other major cities. Then write a three- or four- paragraph essay on unique aspects or special issues facing that country that might cause people to leave as immigrants.

2 SOUTH AMERICA: FROM THE AMAZON TO THE ANDES

South America—the name conjures the sunny beaches of Rio de Janeiro and the fabled temples of Machu Picchu, the loincloth-clad hunters of the Amazon and the leather-wearing gauchos of the pampas. It's a land of magical realism, of mystery and of laughter. In South America one can find gated communities where the wealthy dine on the latest cuisine and imported wines. A visitor can shop in shining new malls for the latest musical release of Britney Spears or Eminem, or head to the theater to take in the most recent Hollywood blockbuster. Travelers can go to Internet cafés to send e-mails to their friends around the world. They can explore the nightlife, perhaps at a discoteca with flashing strobe lights and deafening music, perhaps at an opera house that features the most divine of divas.

And then they can step outside and find children selling chewing gum and shining shoes to pay for that night's meager meal. Or they can hop on a bus and find themselves in a tin-and-cardboard shantytown on the edge of the city where thousands of people survive by picking through the mountains of trash to find rags and bits of salvage to sell.

South America is above all a land of extremes, where the richest 10 percent of the people live quite well on 40 percent of their countries' wealth. Meanwhile, millions survive on less than

◀ A marvel of Inca engineering and building skill, the fortress city of Machu Picchu perches on a mountaintop high above Peru's Urubamba River. Abandoned after the Spanish conquest of the 16th century, Machu Picchu remained undiscovered until 1911.

$1.25 a day. The costs of this inequality are becoming ever more evident.

Colombia

Perhaps more than any other country in South America, Colombia's essence captures the beating heart of the continent. From the Nobel Prize–winning literature of Gabriel García Márquez to the passionate top-40 hits of Shakira, Colombians have made their mark on the world.

The country, home to more than 48.5 million people, is about the size of Texas and Oklahoma combined. Connected to the Central American isthmus by Panama, its boasts beautiful beaches on both the Caribbean and the Pacific, and it also claims dramatic Amazonian and Andean landscapes. Colombia's Caribbean coast still bears 500-year-old signs of the slave trade that formed the beginnings of its economy. The cavernous colonial-era buildings in Cartagena, erected to house the incoming slaves and put them on the auction block, have since been converted into tourist shopping malls. The six-foot-thick walls surrounding the old colonial section of that fabled coastal city are pockmarked from cannonballs shot from the ship of the English privateer Sir Francis Drake. Nestled in the Andes Mountains farther inland is another famous colonial city:

 Words to Understand in This Chapter

campesino—a peasant, or a person from the countryside, who generally makes his or her living from the land.

cassava—a root crop common in South America and other tropical countries. In Spanish, it is called "yuca" (pronounced "you-cah")" It's also referred to in other countries as "manioc." In North America, it is used to make tapioca.

mestizo—a person of mixed indigenous and Spanish heritage.

pre-Columbian—before the time of Christopher Columbus's arrival in the New World.

squatter—a person who settles illegally on unoccupied land.

Decades of violence involving the army, revolutionary guerrillas, right-wing paramilitary groups, and drug cartels have uprooted as many as 2 million Colombians. Here government soldiers supervise the evacuation of villagers caught in the middle of fighting in the Putumayo department, a coca-producing region along Colombia's border with Ecuador.

Popayán. Each year, the city's Holy Week pageants draw colorfully dressed crowds of a quarter million. On Easter the crowds dance in the streets and celebrate the resurrection of Jesus Christ.

Since the 1960s, bloody fighting has raged in Colombia for more than four decades. For years the conflict was confined to the countryside, but in the late 1980s and early 1990s, the violence began to reach the cities, peaking in the mid-2000s. Several generations of children have grown up with bombings, murders, kidnappings, political assassinations, and occasional mortar attacks as facts of life.

Colombia's conflict is complicated and, at times, confusing. Marxist revolutionary groups—the largest of which is the Fuerzas Armadas Revolucionarias de Colombia (FARC)—are seeking to overthrow the government through guerrilla warfare and terrorism. Opposing the guerrillas are Colombia's armed forces as well as right-wing paramilitary organizations—groups of fighters that, while in theory not directly linked to the government, operated with the tacit approval of Colombia's military and were funded by wealthy landowners. At the same time, Colombia's powerful drug cartels—which control the refining of coca leaf into cocaine—supported, and received protection from, both leftist guerrillas and right-wing paramilitaries.

During the administration of Álvaro Uribe from 2002 to 2010, the Colombian government succeeded in regaining control over large areas of the countryside, and some of the factions fighting in Colombia agreed to disarm. Since 2012 the FARC and the Colombian government have been engaged in peace talks that have achieved some positive results. Uribe, backed by billions in aid from the United States, also waged war on the drug cartels. By 2015, the cartels had been significantly weakened, and Colombia was no longer the world's largest producer of cocaine.

Unfortunately, during this time the Colombian government has resorted to human rights abuses to accomplish its goals, according to the U.S. State Department, the United Nations High Commissioner for Human Rights, and other independent groups such as Amnesty International. But all sides in Colombia have been implicated in abuses. But in recent years things seem to be improving in this regard.

The violence of the civil war and the drug trade have led many Colombians to seek safer homes outside of the country. From 1997 to 2002, when the conflict was near its worst, an estimated 1.2 million Colombians emigrated. Many of them moved to neighboring nations such as Ecuador and Venezuela. But more than 75,000 Colombians seeking peace and economic security made their way to the United States or Canada.

Today, Colombian Americans are the largest group of South Americans in the United States. In each U.S. census since 1970, Colombia has led all South American countries in the number of immigrants living in the United States, with more than 20,000 legally admitted each year. The U.S. Census Bureau estimates that there are more than 1 million Colombian Americans living in the United States as of 2016.

Columbians also make up a fairly large share of Canadian immigrants. Between 2005 and 2010, the country admitted an average of more than 6,000 Colombians a year. However, as conditions have improved in Colombia the number of immigrants to Canada has declined: to 4,366 in 2011, 3,741 in 2012, 3,631 in 2013, and 2,860 in 2014, the most recent year for which data is available.

Peru

The Inca Empire during the 15th and early 16th centuries rivaled any European nation in splendor. In those days, Peru encompassed most of western South America, from southern Colombia to the Andean regions of Chile, Argentina, and Bolivia. The empire's extensive road system, irrigation channels, and mountainside terraces, along with striking cities such as the mountaintop stronghold of Machu Picchu, were a monument to Inca power, ingenuity, and engineering skill.

For all their fame, however, the Incas were just one of many nations that populated the Andean region. They were the inheritors of a long line of advances by Andean civilizations, according to José Carlos Fajardo, a Peruvian professor of Quechua at Stanford University. Long before the Incas came to power, the Andean people were among the first to begin cultivating the seeds that would later form the basis for much of the world's diet. Potatoes and pumpkins originated in the Andes, and some historians believe that some early corn and tomato varieties originated there as well.

Andean civilizations were known as well for their scientific knowledge; archaeologists have found evidence that Inca and Wari surgeons performed brain operations—and their patients survived. *Pre-Columbian* metallurgists were working platinum, which the Spaniards called "white gold," before the Europeans learned how. And along with the Aztecs and Mayans of Mesoamerica, the Incas had an understanding of astronomy that matched, if not exceeded, that of their European counterparts.

Everything changed with the Spanish conquest. More than 400 years have passed since Francisco Pizarro's men marched from the Ecuadorian coast inland to Cajamarca, where they seized the Inca emperor Atahualpa. With their horses and their steel weapons, the conquistadors were a devastating foe for the Indians, who were slaughtered by the thousands. After collecting a room full of silver and a room full of gold as ransom, Pizarro had Atahualpa executed, thereby putting an end to the Inca Empire.

The Spaniards quickly plundered the region's gold and silver, melting generations of skillfully wrought artisanry into bars and shipping them back to Spain. The population was soon decimated by epidemics of European illnesses such as smallpox, to which the indigenous people had never been exposed and had no natural immunity. Those who survived were put to work in the region's gold and silver mines, where their lives were often short and filled with suffering.

The Peru of today is home to an enormously diverse population of more than 31 million. About the size of Alaska, Peru is more like several countries within a country, as Peruvian American journalist Sara Fajardo explains. The coastal culture, most notably the capital city of Lima, has dominated the rest of the country economically since the Spanish conquest. But other areas in the remote interior have been able to retain strong cultures that are quite different from those of the coastal peoples. Most notably, there are the indigenous Quechua people of the Andes, who in language and lifestyle have more in common with the people of neighboring Bolivia than with the coastal *Limeñans*. And in the Amazon jungles, thousands of people still retain their tribal ways.

Peruvians today are haunted by the burden of their former glory. They share the plight of most Latin Americans in making do with a second-rate industrial base and an agricultural economy rocked by a shaky world market.

As elsewhere throughout Latin America, many Peruvians take comfort in the biblical admonition to lay up their treasures in the spiritual world. Peruvians are a deeply spiritual people, and in Andean communities, as elsewhere in Latin America, Catholicism blends with indigenous beliefs. The colonial city of Ayacucho boasts 33 churches—one for each year of the life of Christ.

But Peruvians are also masters at another deeply held tradition: recreation. Their deep Catholicism is no impediment to having fun. On the contrary, the feast day of a favorite saint is an excuse for a lavish party or, in some cases, a community festival.

While most city-dwellers wear Western dress in the latest styles, they still take great pride in the country's rich and colorful cultural heritage. You can tell the region of an indigenous person's birth by the intricate stitchery of the women's shawls or the type of hats they wear. And everyone knows the difference between the haunting music of the Andean people, with the *zampoña* (pan pipes) and *charango* (small guitar), and the Spanish-influenced *música criolla* from the coast.

"The Andean perception of the world is not white and black; there's a strong respect for heritage, and each group is proud to have its particularities," said José Carlos Fajardo. "That doesn't mean not to respect the others; they enjoy the others, as well."

Like Colombia, Peru suffered through a long and brutal civil conflict. Peru's civil unrest, which began in the rural province of Ayacucho, had roots in centuries of grievances against the mostly **mestizo** and white ruling elites by the nation's impoverished indigenous population. In 1980 the repressed rage exploded in a campaign of terror undertaken by a revolutionary group intent on overthrowing the government. That group, the Sendero Luminoso (Shining Path), was led by a philosophy professor named Abimael Guzmán and drew its inspiration from the Chinese communist Mao Zedong. A rival group, the much smaller and Marxist-oriented Tupac Amaru Revolutionary Movement, began its own bloody campaign three years later.

In the countryside, the revolutionary groups tried to enlist the support of **campesinos** for their "people's war." Those who resisted were often brutally killed; sometimes whole villages

Buildings in Portoviejo, Ecuador, show the damage caused by a powerful earthquake in April 2016.

were destroyed and all their inhabitants massacred. In the cities, Shining Path and Tupac Amaru tactics included kidnappings, bombings, and assassinations.

For its part, the Peruvian army and police—along with their paramilitary allies—responded harshly. Thousands of Peruvians suspected of supporting the revolutionaries were arrested and tortured. More than 6,000 civilians are believed to have been "disappeared" by police, army, and paramilitary units.

By the early 1990s, the government of President Alberto Fujimori had begun to get the upper hand on the revolutionaries. In 1992 Shining Path leader Abimael Guzmán was captured. By this time, however, the fighting—which would drag on until the end of the decade—had devastated Peru's countryside.

An official report released in August 2003 by Peru's Truth and Reconciliation Commission concluded that the conflict claimed the lives of more than 69,000 people, the majority of them campesinos. Another 600,000 Peruvians were uprooted from their homes.

Even Lima was changed by the bloody war. Tens of thousands of Andean people, and a smaller but still substantial number of people from the Amazon, migrated to the capital to escape the violence and to find employment. The outskirts of Lima now are home to villages of people who are trying to re-create the atmosphere and community of their hometowns. A tour of these *"pueblos jovenes,"* or young villages, is like a miniature tour of the country. Canto Grande, for example, is home to thousands of natives of Ayacucho province. Many of these villages are a collection of dirt-road shanties that until recently lacked even the basic public services of water and sewage. Crime is high and educational opportunities are scant. But one can still hear the music of the Andes in the dusty town plaza as the sun goes down in Canto Grande, and the crispy aroma of the traditional breads of the highlands scents the air of the narrow streets.

Despite recent improvements in the political situation and despite economic improvement in recent years, Peru continues to face significant problems. To cite a particularly sobering example, about one-third of Peru's people are believed to live below the poverty line. Thus a significant number of Peruvians continue to immigrate to North America (12,370 legal immigrants were admitted into the United States in 2013, the most recent year for which complete data is available). Immigration to Canada is less common, with between 700 to 1,900 Peruvians becoming legal Canadian residents each year between 2005 and 2014.

Ecuador

Ecuador is a popular destination for tourists, who wax ecstatic about its towering peaks, its jungles, its colonial cities, and its colorful folkloric traditions. It's also a hot spot for biodiversity, with intact cloud forests and the Galápagos Islands, where the young Charles Darwin's observations led to his later theory of evolution.

But while visitors to Ecuador have the luxury of basking in its beauty, many of the country's 16.3 million people struggle to survive. Tucked between Peru and Colombia on South America's Pacific coast, Ecuador has not experienced as much political violence as its two neighbors, but it has experienced economic turmoil over the past two decades.

Ecuador's economy, which is heavily dependent on agricultural exports, has been struggling for several decades. Increased competition has left the country with declining values for its leading crops, which include bananas, cacao, and coffee.

The discovery of oil in the 1970s brought a decade of prosperity and great wealth to the upper classes. But the oil money eventually also caused economic chaos as well, as prices went up for everyone, including the majority who benefited little from oil revenues. Ecuador invested little in education or infrastructure, so it never developed a strong industrial base. Natural disasters, such as flood and earthquakes, have affected the country's already-weak economy, as has repayment of Ecuador's national debt.

The development of the country's oil reserves made Ecuador the second-leading oil producer in Latin America, after Venezuela. In 2015, oil accounted for 40 percent of Ecuador's exports. The development of the oil industry has helped Ecuador cut its poverty rate from about 40 percent in 1999 to roughly 17.4 percent in 2015. However, this is still a high rate, especially among the indigenous peoples.

As with Peru, indigenous influences are strong in Ecuador: some 8 in 10 Ecuadorians claim Amerindian or mestizo ancestry. Afro-Ecuadorians cluster in the coastal cities, while the descendants of the Spaniards live mostly in the highlands, many of them with vast plantations that are cultivated by indigenous people.

Many emigrants from Ecuador have gone to Europe, chiefly Spain, where an anti-immigrant backlash has ensued. But significant numbers of Ecuadorians have been coming to the United States and Canada as well. The U.S. typically admits about

11,000 Ecuadorians per year as legal residents, the third-largest figure from South America. In 2013, the most recent year for which immigration data is available from the Department of Homeland Security, 10,553 Ecuadorians were admitted as legal residents.

Ecuadorians are far less likely to emigrate to Canada. Between 2005 and 2014, the annual number admitted as legal permanent residents ranged from 282 to 525. In 2014, the most recent year for which data is available, 334 Ecuadorians were admitted to Canada.

Guyana

Guyana, the only English-speaking country on the South American continent, falls into an entirely different category. The tiny country, tucked in between Venezuela and Suriname on South America's Atlantic coast, more closely resembles Jamaica in its culture than it does its South American neighbors. But Guyana also differs from most of the Caribbean countries because of its large East Indian population. More than half of all Guyanese are of East Indian descent; blacks account for an additional 35 to 40 percent of the country's population. A small remnant of the region's indigenous people still live in Guyana, but most have moved to the country's remote interior, and they do not have a visible presence in the country's political life.

The Dutch were the first Europeans to colonize the area. They developed extensive sugar plantations, importing thousands of slaves from Africa to work on the plantations. After the French occupied Holland in 1789, the Dutch turned over the administration of the area to the British, who called it British Guiana.

After slavery was abolished in the British Empire in 1833, the English plantation owners began importing thousands of indentured workers from India. (Indentured workers agree to work for an employer for a specified period of time in exchange for their transportation and food.) The freed slaves established villages and moved to the cities, and a black professional class gradually developed. Meanwhile, the Indians—Hindus as well as Muslims—tended to remain in the rural areas and work on the sugar plantations even after fulfilling their indenture contracts.

To this day, the tiny country of just over 700,000 has sharp divisions between its East Indian and black populations. Blacks maintained political control for most of the 1970s and '80s and into the early '90s. Despite the fact that people of East Indian descent make up the majority of the population, they have been on the political margins for much of the country's history.

Partly because of their exclusion from the political and public life of the country, and partly because of extensive poverty, many Indo-Guyanese immigrated to other Guyanese communities around the world. The exodus, which began during the 1970s, was so large and constant that the population of Guyana did not grow for three decades.

"Migration took our best people," Pundit Reepu Daman Persaud told the magazine *Hinduism Today*. Another Guyanese activist, who declined to give his name, told the magazine, "Our best artists, dancers, singers, musicians left for greener pastures because they simply could not make a living producing Indian culture in a country where the political directorate was hostile to Indian culture."

Brazil

Brazil, a massive country that dominates the eastern part of South America, borders every nation on the continent except Chile and Ecuador. Nearly as large as the United States and home to more than 204 million people, Brazil is a mostly tropical land through which flows the Amazon River, which holds more water than the Nile, the Mississippi, and the Yangtze Rivers put together. Today Brazil has South America's largest economy, as well as a stable, democratically elected government. Brazilians currently make up the fourth-largest group of South American immigrants to the United States.

Brazil continues to be plagued by an extremely unequal distribution of wealth, massive poverty, and widespread landlessness. A look at the statistics presents a stark picture. According

In 2010 Dilma Rousseff became the first woman to serve as president of Brazil, and she was re-elected in 2014. However, reports surfaced that she and other high-ranking government officials had been implicated in a corruption scandal involving Petrobras, the Brazilian oil company. Rousseff underwent impeachment proceedings in 2016.

to an estimate by the U.S. Central Intelligence Agency, Brazil's wealthiest 10 percent shared nearly half (48 percent) of the country's total income; meanwhile, the poorest 10 percent received just 0.7 percent of the income. Many of Brazil's poor are extremely poor: an estimated 50 million live on less than $1.25 a day.

Incomes are highest in the nation's industrialized south-central parts, and lowest in the mainly agricultural northeast, where many *squatters* grow *cassava*. The central state of Minas Gerais is by far the largest source of Brazilian immigrants in the United States. An estimated 40 to 60 percent of the U.S. Brazilian population comes from that state, and a large portion of those people come through a single city—Governador Valadares.

Between 2000 and 2009, 115,404 Brazilians became legal permanent residents of the United States. This was the third-highest figure among all South American countries, trailing only Colombia (236,570) and Peru (137,614). The U.S. admitted 12,057 Brazilians in 2010, 11,643 in 2011, 11,248 in 2012, and

10,772 in 2013. As with other South American countries, Brazilians emigrate to Canada in much smaller numbers. Since 2010, Canada has admitted between 1,915 and 2,598 per year.

Venezuela

Venezuela can boast a little bit of everything South American—the Amazon, the Andes, the cloud forest, the pampas-like llanos, and the sunny Caribbean coast. Above all, however, Venezuela is a Caribbean country, filled with easy-going, affectionate people who laugh easily and know how to have a good time.

The dramatic Venezuelan landscapes are a source of great pride to its people, from snow-capped Mérida in the Andes to the strange, flat-topped peaks in the Gran Sabana of the southeast. Angel Falls, the world's tallest waterfall, cascades from the top of one of these *tepuis*, as they're called, and tourists from around the world pay hundreds of dollars apiece to fly in and get a look at it. About twice the size of California, Venezuela dominates the northernmost coast of South America; it has a population of 30.6 million.

Venezuela's political and economic reality these days is dominated by oil. After the discovery of new oilfields in the 1970s, the country experienced a brief euphoria and a period of economic prosperity—though, as always, the lower class and poor benefited little. Oil prices dropped in the late 1980s, plunging the country into crisis when hundreds of thousands of people were thrown out of work. Riots swept through Caracas and were violently repressed, and two coup attempts took place in 1992.

In December 1998, Venezuelans signaled their impatience with the government's inability to restore order and national pride by electing a fierce populist, Hugo Chávez, to the presidency with the largest vote margin in 40 years. Just six years earlier, Chávez had attempted a coup against the government, for which he had spent two years in jail. In 2000 Chávez was reelected for a six-year term, again by a comfortable margin.

But Chávez created turmoil with his authoritarian ways. A

Venezuelan leader Hugo Chávez was a fierce critic of the United States. The U.S. government, in turn, strongly opposed his socialist policies in Venezuela.

three-day general strike ended in a violent demonstration in April 2002, during which Chávez's snipers killed 12 people. After the incident, the military arrested Chávez. But demands by Western governments that Venezuela remain loyal to its constitution led to Chávez's reinstatement as president 48 hours later.

Chávez remained under pressure throughout the year. In December 2002 a general strike, undertaken to protest the president's policies, crippled the vital oil industry, cutting production to about one-third. Government spending curbed the strike's effects, but Venezuela stayed divided over Chávez. He was reelected for a third term in 2006, and for a fourth term in 2012.

However, by this time Chávez was suffering from cancer, and he died of the disease in 2013 before he could be inaugurated. He had recommended a close ally, Nicolás Maduro, succeed him. In a special election in April 2013, Maduro was elected president of Venezuela.

In 2014, Venezuelans began holding protests throughout the country about the country's high levels of urban violence, high inflation rate, and chronic shortages of basic goods. Venezuela had slipped into an economic recession by this point, exacerbating the problem. The protests have continued into 2016.

Immigration from Venezuela to the United States has held fairly steady over the past decade, at about 9,500 people per year. In 2013, 9,512 Venezuelans were granted legal permanent residence in the U.S. Between 1,000 and 1,500 Venezuelans typically emigrate to Canada, with 1,483 being legally admitted to the country in 2014.

Argentina

Argentina, together with neighboring countries Uruguay and Chile, makes up a cultural group that in many ways is more similar to Europe than to the rest of South America. Most Latin American countries have a large mestizo population. But 85 percent of Argentina's 43 million citizens are white; most are of Italian or Spanish origin, although a significant number are the descendants of German, French, or British immigrants.

One of the continent's most developed countries, Argentina has the largest middle class in Latin America and an education level similar to the United States and Europe. The sophisticated drama of the Argentine tango flavors the brightly lit and bustling nights of downtown Buenos Aires, "the Paris of Latin America."

But Argentina is much more than Buenos Aires. The second-largest country in South America, it stretches from the Tierra del Fuego at the icy southern tip of the continent northward through Patagonia and the vast, flat pampas, all the way to the steamy jungles of the Chaco state. To the west, along the border with Chile, are the rugged Andes Mountains. In total area Argentina is about the size of the United States east of the Mississippi River.

Argentina's countryside developed much like the Old West of the United States. The gauchos became the symbol of the cowboy frontier of the pampas. Like their northern counterparts, they developed a rich folklore of music and legend that has influenced the national culture. Argentines drink their *maté* (pronounced "mah-TAY") with pride from leather-covered cups inspired by those the gauchos have sipped around the campfire for generations. Recently U.S. companies have begun to popularize the drink in the United States as a healthful alternative to coffee.

In 1900 Argentina was one of the world's 10 richest countries. But at the end of the 20th century, with a legacy of brutal war and repression, corrupt governments, and a mismanaged economy, 40 percent of the nation's people were living in poverty. Half of the country's 15 million poor have fallen from the middle class since 1985. In 2002 a survey showed that a third of the country's people would leave if they could. That year Argentina defaulted on its $155 billion foreign debt. The government's devaluation of the Argentine peso upended the banking industry and wiped out middle-class savings. Nearly 300,000 people left the country.

In 2003, Peronist Néstor Kirchner was elected president. He improved relations with other Latin American nations and restructured foreign debt. The economy recovered considerably, but the authority Kirchner gave himself caused some worry. Kirchner's wife, Cristina Fernández de Kirchner, became the next president in 2007. Thanks to strong economic growth during her term, she was elected to a second term as president in 2011.

However, some of the growth turned out to be a mirage. In 2013, the World Bank censured Argentina for not providing accurate data about the rate of inflation and economic growth. And by 2015, with Argentina having trouble paying back its international debt, the economy had once again fallen into crisis.

Compared with other South American countries, immigration from Argentina to the United States is relatively low. Between 2000 and 2009, 47,955 Argentines became legal permanent residents of the U.S.—an average of less than 5,000 a year. In 2012 and 2013, Argentina sent 4,218 and 4,227 people to the U.S. The same is true of Canada, where fewer than 300 Argentines became legal permanent residents each year between 2011 and 2014.

Chile

Strung like a pearl necklace between the Pacific and the Andes,

narrow Chile extends more than half the length of South America. Its mostly white, European population of 18 million is, along with those of Argentina and Uruguay, among the most educated in the world.

After a brutal dictatorship that lasted nearly two decades, Chile is enjoying a period of relative calm and prosperity. Compared with its neighbors, Chile is an island of stability. The country has instituted a number of important economic reforms in the past decade and has followed a road of fiscal frugality that seems to have paid off. While Argentina was racking up huge debts with the International Monetary Fund, Chile took advantage of a global surge in copper prices to bolster its reserves. Today, one economist called Chile "the Ireland of Latin America," drawing parallels between the two countries' leap from poverty to a place at the table with major world trading partners.

But it wasn't always this way. On September 11, 1973, a bloody coup deposed, and claimed the life of, Chile's popular-

A refined, cosmopolitan city of more than 12 million, Buenos Aires earned the nickname "the Paris of Latin America." But in recent years Argentina's financial problems have cast a pall over the capital.

ly elected president, Salvador Allende. The military junta that took control, which was headed by General Augusto Pinochet (who later declared himself president), immediately began rounding up, torturing, and killing Allende supporters and those believed to have "subversive" leanings. These included government employees, trade unionists, factory workers, students, artists, and socialists and communists. Over the next 15 years, tens of thousands of Chileans were tortured, and more than 3,000 were murdered or "disappeared." During this time, many of Chile's most famous intellectuals, artists, musicians, and writers fled the country, joining the thousands of ordinary citizens who left to escape the regime. Some were not able to return home for more than two decades.

In 1988 a plebiscite was held to determine Chile's political future, and Pinochet lost. The following year free elections were held, and Pinochet was forced to relinquish the presidency in 1990. However, he retained enormous power over the country as head of the Chilean military. Not until Pinochet retired in 1998 did many exiled Chileans begin to feel it was safe for them to return home. That same year, the former dictator was arrested in England in connection with human rights violations. After a big international legal battle, he was returned to Chile, where he was judged to be too elderly and infirm to stand trial. This decision was later overturned, but Pinochet died in 2006 without being convicted of any crimes.

In the 1988 plebiscite, Chileans voted for elections to choose a new president and the majority of members of a two-chamber congress. On December 14, 1989, Christian Democrat Patricio Aylwin, the candidate of a coalition of 17 political parties, received an absolute majority of votes. President Aylwin served from 1990 to 1994. In December 1993, Christian Democrat Eduardo Frei Ruiz-Tagle (the son of former president Eduardo Frei-Montalva), replaced Aylwin as president. He would serve a six-year term, instead of four years, as a result of a change to the constitution in 1997. The presidential election held on December 12, 1999, failed to produce a majority for any of the six candidates, which led to an unprecedented runoff election on January 16, 2000. Ricardo Lagos Escobar of the Socialist Party and the Party for Democracy won a narrow victory, with 51.32 percent of the votes. During his six-year presidency, Lagos earned consistently high approval ratings.

In 2005, Michelle Bachelet, also a member of the Socialist Party, became Chile's first woman president following a runoff. Bachelet and her parents had been imprisoned and tortured during the Pinochet dictatorship, and as president, she promised to make social justice a priority.

In February 2010, Chile was struck by an earthquake that measured 8.8 on the Richter scale, making it the fifth-largest earthquake ever recorded to that point. The offshore quake caused a tsuname that destroyed hundreds of thousands of homes and killed more than 500 people.

Bachelet lost the 2009 presidential election to Sebastián Piñera, which resulted in a peaceful transfer of power to the opposition National Renewal party. However, Bachelet was elected to another term as president in 2013, receiving more than 62 percent of the vote.

Compared to other South American countries, Chile sends relatively few immigrants to the United States. Only 1,751 Chileans became legal permanent residents of the U.S. in 2013, while just 299 became residents of Canada in 2014.

Uruguay

Uruguay is a small but proud country that, for much of its history, has thrived in the shadow of its larger neighbors, Argentina and Brazil. Slightly smaller than the state of Washington, it is home to about 3.3 million people. Uruguay is a temperate country, with winter temperatures rarely reaching the freezing point. Its beaches were once a haven for Argentine tourists, and its grasslands sustained cattle herds that helped satisfy the Argentine taste for beef.

Like its neighbor Argentina, Uruguay in recent years has experienced an economic crisis. Many observers blame

Argentina for its own economic woes, pointing to a spendthrift government and a huge international debt. But few point the finger at Uruguay, whose rock-solid banking institutions and responsible fiscal policies earned it a reputation as "the Switzerland of South America." Most economists agree that tiny Uruguay was a hapless victim, pulled down like a sapling in the mighty crash of its much larger neighbor. Even Brazil, with one of the world's largest economies, was severely shaken by Argentina's economic collapse. Uruguay, struggling desperately to keep its financial institutions upright in the midst of the regional crisis, saw a run on its banks in early 2002 that ended with a severe banking crisis in August of that year. Many of the depositors rushing to pull out their money were Argentines. The Uruguayan peso collapsed, and so did four national banks. Inflation soared, leaving wages worth 11 percent less in 2002 than they had been the year before. Overall, 2002 saw the Uruguayan economy contract by an estimated 10.5 percent.

The U.S. government granted Uruguay a $1.5 billion short-term loan to help stabilize its economy. But investor confidence in the region's institutions remained severely shaken. Nonetheless, immigration from Uruguay to the United States remains low. Only 9,827 people from Uruguay became legal permanent residents of the U.S. between 2000 and 2009, and since then immigration has averaged about 1,400 per year. Since 2009, fewer than 100 Uruguayans per year have sought permanent residence in Canada.

 Text-Dependent Questions

1. What South American country provides the largest number of immigrants to the United States annually?
2. What has been occurring in Venezuela since 2014? Why?

 Research Project

Using library resources or the Internet, find out more about Argentina's financial crisis of 1998-2002. List the five most surprising things you learned.

3 IMMIGRATION TO NORTH AMERICA

South Americans, like all Latin Americans, have been struggling to gain a better life through immigration since the late 1800s. Overall, however, the numbers of South Americans immigrating to the United States remained relatively small until 1960–1969. During that decade, 250,754 people from South America became legal permanent residents of the U.S., compared to fewer than 80,000 during the 1950s. That nearly three-fold increase was followed by another slight rise in 1970–1979 (to 273,529), then by another dramatic increase during the "Lost Decade" of the 1980s, when many South Americans were fleeing violence or economic crises in their homelands. Beween 1980 and 1989, almost 400,000 people from South America became legal permanent residents of the U.S. Immigration from South America has continued to rise, with 570,596 coming to America during the 1990s, and 856,508 coming in the period 2000 to 2009. In the past five years, around 80,000 people from South America have emigrated to the United States annually.

To a certain extent, fluctuations in the immigration numbers reflect changing conditions and specific events occurring in South America over time: the rise or fall of dictatorships, wars, earthquakes and other natural disasters, economic circum-

◄A Hispanic immigrant participates in a rally for immigration reform in Arizona. Over the past decade, more than 850,000 immigrants from South America have been granted legal permanent residence in the United States.

stances. But immigration is also affected by laws and policies in the destination countries. To place immigration from South America in context, it is useful to look briefly at the history of U.S. and Canadian immigration.

A Short History of U.S. Immigration

Immigration to the United States has been characterized by openness punctuated by periods of restriction. During the 17th, 18th, and 19th centuries, immigration was essentially open without restriction, and, at times, immigrants were even recruited to come to America. Between 1783 and 1820, approximately 250,000 immigrants arrived at U.S. shores. Between 1841 and 1860, more than 4 million immigrants came; most were from England, Ireland, and Germany.

Historically, race and ethnicity have played a role in legislation to restrict immigration. The Chinese Exclusion Act of 1882, which was not repealed until 1943, specifically prevented Chinese people from becoming U.S. citizens and did not allow Chinese laborers to immigrate for the next decade. An agreement with Japan in the early 1900s prevented most Japanese immigration to the United States.

Until the 1920s, no numerical restrictions on immigration existed in the United States, although health restrictions applied. The only other significant restrictions came in 1917, when passing a literacy test became a requirement for immigrants. Presidents Cleveland, Taft, and Wilson had vetoed similar meas-

 Words to Understand in This Chapter

deportation—forced removal of someone from a country, usually back to his or her native land.

eugenics—the study, now derided as a false science, of attempting to "improve" the human race through breeding; often used as a cover for racial discrimination.

visa—official authorization that permits arrival at a port of entry but does not guarantee admission into the United States.

A satirical cartoon entitled "A Statue for *Our* Harbor," printed in an 1881 issue of the San Francisco–based magazine *The Wasp*, represents the anti-immigration perspective of many Americans during the 19th century. The cartoon attributes a number of social problems, including immorality, disease, filth, and the ruin of "white labor," to Chinese immigrants. The drawing appeared a year before Congress passed the Chinese Exclusion Act of 1882, which prohibited the Chinese from immigrating to the United States.

A STATUE FOR *OUR* HARBOR.

ures earlier. In addition, in 1917 a prohibition was added to the law against the immigration of people from Asia (defined as the Asiatic barred zone). While a few of these prohibitions were lifted during World War II, they were not repealed until 1952, and even then Asians were only allowed in under very small annual quotas.

U.S. Immigration Policy from World War I to 1965

During World War I, the federal government required that all travelers to the United States obtain a *visa* at a U.S. consulate or diplomatic post abroad. As former State Department consular affairs officer C. D. Scully points out, by making that requirement permanent Congress, by 1924, established the framework of temporary, or non-immigrant visas (for study, work, or travel), and immigrant visas (for permanent residence). That framework remains in place today.

After World War I, cultural intolerance and bizarre racial theories led to new immigration restrictions. The House Judiciary Committee employed a *eugenics* consultant, Dr. Harry

N. Laughlin, who asserted that certain races were inferior. Another leader of the eugenics movement, Madison Grant, argued that Jews, Italians, and others were inferior because of their supposedly different skull size.

The Immigration Act of 1924, preceded by the Temporary Quota Act of 1921, set new numerical limits on immigration based on "national origin." Taking effect in 1929, the 1924 act set annual quotas on immigrants that were specifically designed to keep out southern Europeans, such as Italians and Greeks. Generally no more than 100 people of the proscribed nationalities were permitted to immigrate.

While the new law was rigid, the U.S. Department of State's restrictive interpretation directed consular officers overseas to be even stricter in their application of the "public charge" provision. (A public charge is someone unable to support himself or his family.) As author Laura Fermi wrote, "In response to the

Before changes in the immigration laws that occurred during the 1960s, most immigrants to the United States and Canada came from the countries of Europe.

new cry for restriction at the beginning of the [Great Depression] . . . the consuls were to interpret very strictly the clause prohibiting admission of aliens 'likely to become public charges; and to deny the visa to an applicant who in their opinion might become a public charge at any time.'"

In the early 1900s, more than one million immigrants a year came to the United States. In 1930—the first year of the national-origin quotas—approximately 241,700 immigrants were admitted. But under the State Department's strict interpretations, only 23,068 immigrants entered during 1933, the smallest total since 1831. Later these restrictions prevented many Jews in Germany and elsewhere in Europe from escaping what would become the Holocaust. At the height of the Holocaust in 1943, the United States admitted fewer than 6,000 refugees.

The Displaced Persons Act of 1948, the nation's first refugee law, allowed many refugees from World War II to settle in the United States. The law put into place policy changes that had already seen immigration rise from 38,119 in 1945 to 108,721 in 1946 (and later to 249,187 in 1950). One-third of those admitted between 1948 and 1951 were Poles, with ethnic Germans forming the second-largest group.

The 1952 Immigration and Nationality Act is best known for its restrictions against those who supported communism or anarchy. However, the bill's other provisions were quite restrictive and were passed over the veto of President Truman. The 1952 act retained the national-origin quota system for the Eastern Hemisphere. The Western Hemisphere continued to operate without a quota and relied on other qualitative factors to limit immigration. Moreover, during that time, the Mexican bracero program, from 1942 to 1964, allowed millions of Mexican agricultural workers to work temporarily in the United States.

The 1952 act set aside half of each national quota to be divided among three preference categories for relatives of U.S. citizens and permanent residents. The other half went to aliens with high education or exceptional abilities. These quotas applied only to those from the Eastern Hemisphere.

A Halt to the National-Origin Quotas

The Immigration and Nationality Act of 1965 became a land-mark in immigration legislation by specifically striking the racially based national-origin quotas. It removed the barriers to Asian immigration, which later led to opportunities to immigrate for many Filipinos, Chinese, Koreans, and others. The Western Hemisphere was designated a ceiling of 120,000 immigrants but without a preference system or per country limits. Modifications made in 1978 ultimately combined the Western and Eastern Hemispheres into one preference system and one ceiling of 290,000.

The 1965 act built on the existing system—without the national-origin quotas—and gave somewhat more priority to family relationships. It did not completely overturn the existing system but rather carried forward essentially intact the family immigration categories from the 1959 amendments to the

The 1965 Immigration and Nationality Act, signed by President Lyndon Johnson, was one of the century's most significant immigration acts. With its employment preferences and priorities granted to family members, the act created resettlement opportunities for thousands of newcomers from India and other Asian countries.

Immigration and Nationality Act. Even though the text of the law prior to 1965 indicated that half of the immigration slots were reserved for skilled employment immigration, in practice, Immigration and Naturalization Service (INS) statistics show that 86 percent of the visas issued between 1952 and 1965 went for family immigration.

A number of significant pieces of legislation since 1980 have shaped the current U.S. immigration system. First, the Refugee Act of 1980 removed refugees from the annual world limit and established that the president would set the number of refugees who could be admitted each year after consultations with Congress.

Second, the 1986 Immigration Reform and Control Act (IRCA) introduced sanctions against employers who "knowingly" hired undocumented immigrants (those here illegally). It also provided amnesty for many undocumented immigrants.

Third, the Immigration Act of 1990 increased legal immigration by 40 percent. In particular, the act significantly increased the number of employment-based immigrants (to 140,000), while also boosting family immigration.

Fourth, the 1996 Illegal Immigration Reform and Immigrant Responsibility Act (IIRAIRA) significantly tightened rules that permitted undocumented immigrants to convert to legal status and made other changes that tightened immigration law in areas such as political asylum and *deportation*.

Fifth, in response to the September 11, 2001, terrorist attacks, the USA PATRIOT Act and the Enhanced Border Security and Visa Entry Reform Act tightened rules on the granting of visas to individuals from certain countries and enhanced the federal government's monitoring and detention authority over foreign nationals in the United States.

New U.S. Immigration Agencies

In a dramatic reorganization of the federal government, the Homeland Security Act of 2002 abolished the Immigration and Naturalization Service and transferred its immigration service

President Bush signs the Enhanced Border Security and Visa Entry Reform Act with congressional members in attendance, May 2002. The act, along with the USA PATRIOT Act, was passed in response to the September 2001 terrorist attacks.

and enforcement functions from the Department of Justice into a new Department of Homeland Security. The Customs Service, the Coast Guard, and parts of other agencies were also transferred into the new department.

The Department of Homeland Security, with regards to immigration, is organized as follows: The bureau of Customs and Border Protection (CBP) contains Customs and Immigration inspectors, who check the documents of travelers to the United States at air, sea, and land ports of entry; and Border Patrol agents, the uniformed agents who seek to prevent unlawful entry along the southern and northern border. The new bureau of Immigration and Customs Enforcement (ICE) employs investigators, who attempt to find undocumented immigrants inside the United States, and Detention and Removal officers, who detain and seek to deport such individuals. The new bureau of Citizenship and Immigration Services (USCIS) is where people go, or correspond with, to become U.S. citizens or obtain permission to work or extend their stay in the United States.

Following the terrorist attacks of September 11, 2001, the Department of Justice adopted several measures that did not require new legislation to be passed by Congress. Some of these measures created controversy and raised concerns about civil liberties. For example, FBI and INS agents detained for months more than 1,000 foreign nationals of Middle Eastern descent and refused to release the names of the individuals. It is alleged that the Department of Justice adopted tactics that discouraged the detainees from obtaining legal assistance. The Department of Justice also began requiring foreign nationals from primarily Muslim nations to be fingerprinted and questioned by immigration officers upon entry or if they have been living in the United States. Those involved in the September 11 attacks were not immigrants—people who become permanent residents with a right to stay in the United States—but holders of temporary visas, primarily visitor or tourist visas.

Immigration to the United States Today

From the 1920s to the 1960s, the rate of legal immigration to the United States was kept low. Since the immigration law changes of the mid-1960s, the number of foreign-born people in the United States has been rising steadily. The foreign-born population was about 9.6 million according to the 1970 census. This was 4.7 percent of the total U.S. population. That number, as well as its proportion to the overall population, has increased in every census since then, rising to 14.1 million (6.2 percent) in 1980, 19.8 million (7.9 percent) in 1990, 31.1 million (11.1 percent) in 2000, and 40 million (12.9 percent) in 2010. That 2010 figure is the highest since 1920, when foreign-born people made up 13.2 percent of the population.

Some people today believe that legal immigration should be restricted again. These people maintain that immigrants take jobs native-born Americans could fill and that U.S. population growth, which immigration contributes to, harms the environment. Thus far, Congress has declined to place additional restrictions on immigration.

Today, the legal immigration system in the United States contains many rules, permitting only individuals who fit into certain categories to immigrate—and in many cases only after waiting anywhere from one to ten years or more, depending on the demand in that category. The system, representing a compromise among family, employment, and human rights concerns, has the following elements:

> A U.S. citizen may sponsor for immigration a spouse, parent, sibling, or minor or adult child.

> A lawful permanent resident (green card holder) may sponsor only a spouse or child.

> A foreign national may immigrate if he or she gains an employer sponsor.

> An individual who can show that he or she has a "well-founded fear of persecution" may come to the country as a refugee—or be allowed to stay as an asylee (someone who receives asylum).

Beyond these categories, essentially the only other way to immigrate is to apply for and receive one of the "diversity" visas, which are granted annually by lottery to those from "underrepresented" countries.

A Short History of Canadian Immigration

In the 1800s, immigration into Canada was largely unrestricted. Farmers and artisans from England and Ireland made up a significant portion of 19th-century immigrants. England's Parliament passed laws that facilitated and encouraged the voyage to North America, particularly for the poor.

After the United States barred Chinese railroad workers from settling in the country, Canada encouraged the immigration of Chinese laborers to assist in the building of Canadian railways. Responding to the racial views of the time, the Canadian Parliament began charging a "head tax" for Chinese and South Asian (Indian) immigrants in 1885. The fee of $50—later raised to $500—was well beyond the means of laborers making one or two dollars a day. Later, the government sought additional ways to prohibit Asians from entering the country. For example, it decided to require a "continuous journey," meaning that immigrants to Canada had to travel from their country on a boat that made an uninterrupted passage. For immigrants or asylum seekers from Asia this was nearly impossible.

As the 20th century progressed, concerns about race led to further restrictions on immigration to Canada. These restrictions particularly hurt Jewish and other refugees seeking to flee persecution in Europe. Government statistics indicate that Canada

 ## Illegal Immigration to the United States

Each year, approximately a million immigrants are legally admitted to the United States. But over the years the undocumented (illegal) portion of the U.S. population has increased. By 2016, the Pew Research Center estimates, approximately 11.3 million undocumented immigrants were living in the United States.

In recent years, the U.S. government has created programs that would help some of these undocumented immigrants to attain legal status within the United States. In June 2012, U.S. President Barack Obama announced a new government policy called Deferred Action for Childhood Arrivals (DACA). Persons who had entered the country illegally before the age of 16, who had lived in the country continuously since June 2007 (later changed to January 1, 2010), and who fulfilled certain other requirements could qualify under DACA, which protected them from being deported back to their parents' country of origin.

In November 2014, President Obama announced another policy, Deferred Action for Parents of Americans and Lawful Permanent Residents, or DAPA. Under DAPA, undocumented immigrants who had lived in the United States continuously since January 1, 2010, and who had children who were U.S. citizens or lawful permanent residents would be exempt from deportation. They could also receive a renewable three-year work permit. However, several states filed lawsuits over DAPA, and in February 2015 a federal court halted the implementation of DAPA pending the outcome of those suits.

In the meantime, the U.S. government has also taken many steps increase security on the borders and prevent illegal immigration. As of 2015, fences lined more than a third of the 1,989-mile (3,200-km) U.S.-Mexico land boundary. In 2015 the Department of Homeland Security requested nearly $13 billion for Customs and Border Protection. In 2002, by comparison, only $5 billion had been allocated for those functions. While there were slightly under 8,600 U.S. Border Patrol agents in 2000, by 2015 that number stood at about 21,000. Those agents patrol the border in trucks and helicopters, on horseback and quad bikes to prevent illegal crossings. In desert areas they may drag car tires to smooth the sand, making it easier to spot footprints. In other areas seismic sensors buried under roads or along well-traveled paths detect the sound of footsteps. Floodlights illuminate fences, and infrared cameras track movements of anyone trying to slip across the border in the darkness. Drones circle overhead constantly.

Some South American professionals—especially those in the medical field—have found that their credentials are not immediately transferable in the U.S. and have thus had to take employment with fewer skill requirements.

accepted no more than 5,000 Jewish refugees before and during the Holocaust.

After World War II, Canada, like the United States, began accepting thousands of Europeans displaced by the war. Canada's laws were modified to accept these war refugees, as well as Hungarians fleeing Communist authorities after the crushing of the 1956 Hungarian Revolution.

The Immigration Act of 1952 in Canada allowed for a "tap on, tap off" approach to immigration, granting administrative authorities the power to allow more immigrants into the country in good economic times, and fewer in times of recession. The shortcoming of such an approach is that there is little evidence immigrants harm a national economy and much evidence they contribute to economic growth, particularly in the growth of the labor force.

In 1966 the government of Prime Minister Lester Pearson introduced a policy statement stressing how immigrants were key to Canada's economic growth. With Canada's relatively small population base, it became clear that in the absence of newcomers, the country would not be able to grow. The policy was introduced four years after Parliament enacted important legislation that eliminated Canada's own version of racially based national-origin quotas.

In 1967 a new law established a points system that awarded entry to potential immigrants using criteria based primarily on an individual's age, language ability, skills, education, family relationships, and job prospects. The total points needed for entry of an immigrant is set by the Minister of Citizenship and Immigration Canada. The new law also established a category for humanitarian (refugee) entry.

The 1976 Immigration Act refined and expanded the possibility for entry under the points system, particularly for those seeking to sponsor family members. The act also expanded refugee and asylum law to comport with Canada's international obligations. The law established five basic categories for immigration into Canada: 1) family; 2) humanitarian; 3) independents (including skilled workers), who immigrate to Canada on their own; 4) assisted relatives; and 5) business immigrants (including investors, entrepreneurs, and the self-employed).

The new Immigration and Refugee Protection Act, which took effect June 28, 2002, made a series of modifications to existing Canadian immigration law. The act, and the regulations that followed, toughened rules on those seeking asylum and the process for removing people unlawfully in Canada.

The law modified the points system, adding greater flexibility for skilled immigrants and temporary workers to become permanent residents, and evaluating skilled workers on the weight of their transferable skills as well as those of their specific occupation. The legislation also made it easier for employers to have a labor shortage declared in an industry or sector, which would facilitate the entry of foreign workers in that industry or sector.

On family immigration, the act permitted parents to sponsor dependent children up to the age of 22 (previously 19 was the maximum age at which a child could be sponsored for immigration). The act also allowed partners in common-law arrangements, including same-sex partners, to be considered as family members for the purpose of immigration sponsorship. Along with these liberalizing measures, the act also included provisions to address perceived gaps in immigration-law enforcement.

Immigration from South America

U.S. government statistics show a rise in legal immigration from South America in each decade of the 20th century, with the exception of 1931–1940—during the Great Depression and the State Department's efforts to keep out would-be immigrants who might become public charges. The number of South American immigrants shot up from fewer than 80,000 in the period 1950–1959 to more than a quarter million for 1960–1969. In the 1990s, more than 570,000 South Americans immigrated to the United States. The period 2000 to 2009 set another record, with 856,508 South Americans becoming permanent residents of the United States. Immigration from South American has continued at this rate, with roughly 80,000 to 85,000 people from the southern continent becoming U.S. residents each year since 2010.

Canada became home to thousands of Chileans and Argentines fleeing the repressive dictatorships of the 1970s, and then in the 1980s to Peruvians fleeing violence from the Shining Path and the military. By 2011, the Canadian census reported that 381,280 residents were immigrants who had been born in Latin America. Mexicans (69,695) were the largest Hispanic immigrant group in Canada, as they are in the United States. Just behind them were immigrants from Colombia, with a population counted at 60,555. Immigrants from El Salvador ranked third, followed by Chile (25,195), Brazil (22,920), Argentina (18,870), and Venezuela (16,005).

The largest immigrant population from South America in Canada was from Guyana, which, as a fellow British Commonwealth nation, has a natural connection to Canada. The 2011 census counted 75,348 Guyanese.

 # Text-Dependent Questions

1. Name the U.S. law that prevented most Asian immigrants from entering the country. When did the law go into effect? When was it repealed?

2. What steps did the Canadian government take to limit immigration before the 1960s?

3. Why did many Indian workers come to the United States during the 1990s?

 # Research Project

Investigate the contribution of foreign laborers to the construction of the Transcontinental Railroad. Write a two-page report.

4 Making a New Life

Many South Americans feel more at home in North America than they did in their home countries. Canada and the United States give them more freedom to be who they are. Sergio Karas, an Argentine immigration lawyer living in Toronto, wouldn't dream of going back. His assessment of his homeland is harsh.

"In order to succeed you have to leave Argentina," he said. "It's sad to say it, but it's true. [Argentina] is a country that stifles you. Why would you do it the right way if the wrong way is more fruitful? Corruption and malfeasance pays, that's the lesson to the children."

But no matter how critical they are of the government of their homeland or even of their own people, there's a part of most South American immigrants that will always look back home with nostalgia. Many dream of going home someday, but for many, that day never comes. Travel home is expensive, and visas back into the United States or Canada are hard to come by, so a choice to return for a visit could be permanent.

For many, returning isn't an option, even if they wanted to. Their families back home, and indeed their countries' economies, have come to count on the money they send. *Remittances*, or the money a person abroad sends back to his or

◀Even as they make new lives for themselves in the United States or Canada, many South American immigrants look toward the countries of their birth with undying nostalgia—and still define themselves not simply as Latinos but as Argentines or Peruvians, Chileans, Colombians, or Uruguayans. This somewhat lighthearted take on national identity in Latino America was photographed in South Florida.

her home country, continue to make up one of the largest sources of income for most Latin American nations. Professionals like Venezuelan dentist Olga Potella, Peruvian public accountant Sylvia Paz, and Uruguayan veterinarian Nancy Malugani have left their careers to take less prestigious jobs in the United States.

"A lot of us succeed, and in some ways, that makes it harder," said Argentine economist Luis Brunstein, who immigrated to the United States as a 22-year-old X-ray technician. Twenty years and a doctoral degree later, he's here to stay. "The opportunity cost of going back becomes so much more expensive, and going back to Argentina to struggle and try to find a job becomes so much more difficult, almost impossible. Those are some of the things we are facing all the time."

Job prospects in Argentina and Uruguay, and in the Andean countries to the north, remain grim, as most South American economies continue on a downward slide. And in the most extreme cases, as in Colombia, returning home could mean kidnapping or even death.

Brazil and Chile are the exception to the rule, with relatively strong economies that, despite some problems, appear to be integrating into the global economy. Together with Mexico, Brazil accounts for two-thirds of Latin America's economic output. But Argentina and Venezuela, two of the wealthiest countries on the continent, are beset by economic and political turmoil.

"More than half of my life has been spent here, but I still

 Words to Understand in This Chapter

assimilation—the process by which a person from one culture takes on the mind-set, customs, and habits of another culture.

brazuca—a Brazilian living in the United States.

paisano—a compatriot, or person from the same country (particularly when in a foreign land).

remittances—money sent back home by immigrants, usually to their families.

hope to go back home," says Brunstein. "Every Argentine I know feels the same; but we never go back, because every year, it's worse."

Re-creating the Feeling of Home

Beyond the deep gratitude, loyalty, and even patriotism that most South American immigrants feel for their new country, there's something missing for them. It's in the taste of their foods, the rhythm in their steps, the warmth in their embraces. It's harder to make meaningful, lasting friendships in North America, some say.

"You cannot really drop by someone's house here, the way we did back home," says Brunstein. "You have to make an appointment. In Argentina, people will drop by and drink maté and bring a pastry, and you talk all afternoon about everything and about nothing. Here, in 25 years, that has not happened once."

For some immigrants, the best way to combat feelings of isolation is to reach out to their fellow countrymen and women and re-create the culture of home. Sometimes it's through cultural events such as the enormous Colombian Independence Day festivals in Miami and New York, which provide a way of sharing beloved aspects of a culture and creating a sense of home. Sometimes it's through a community center or a restaurant. Sometimes it's through sporting events, such as soccer tournaments.

For others, the best way to maintain a connection to their culture is to reach out and help newcomers. Long-established immigrants like Mauricio Hurtado, an accountant from Colombia, work quietly behind the scenes to ease the transition of new immigrants in their area.

Hurtado lives in Missouri, where the past decade has seen a rapid influx of Latino immigrants, mainly Mexicans and Central Americans. He's become a sort of informal referral service for people who run into problems because they don't understand the system. He advocates for families as they work their way through the red tape.

And now, as he approaches retirement from his state government job, Hurtado is gearing up to start a second career: marketing energy-saving devices in Colombian hospitals and other public buildings. At the same time, he's been networking with groups that are collecting used and discarded medical equipment, and working to get the equipment placed in Colombian hospitals.

"People sometimes call me and thank me for what I've done and I say, well, that's OK," says the affable accountant. "But really it feels good—because if they succeed, we all succeed."

Where They Go and What They Do

South American immigrants in general are more likely to live in big cities or in the suburbs rather than in small towns or rural areas—90 percent of those counted in the 2010 U.S. census lived in metropolitan areas of 1 million or more, compared with 65 percent for Mexicans, who are much more widely dispersed. And unlike Mexicans and Central Americans, who tend to live in the Southwest and California, South Americans gravitate to Miami and the East Coast. In Canada, they are more likely to live in Toronto or Montreal, although there are sizable populations (about 10,000 each) in British Columbia and Alberta as well.

By far, the largest numbers of South Americans are concentrated in the New York-New Jersey area. About 847,000 South American immigrants live in this region. Florida is home to the next biggest group, with about 449,000 living in the Miami-Fort Lauderdale region. The Washington, D.C., metropolitan area, which includes Alexandria and Arlington, Virginia, is home to about 135,000 South American immigrants. Another 122,000 live in the Los Angeles-Long Beach-Anaheim areas of California.

An interesting trend has emerged in the past decade: immigrants moving directly to the suburbs. "There's the old classic pattern of two-stage migration, where the lone pioneer immigrant saves up and moves to the suburbs," said Stewart Lawrence, an immigration analyst in Washington, D.C. "Among Latinos, that's no longer the dynamic. There are enough people out in the suburbs now that they go right to the 'burbs."

They go where the jobs are, and increasingly, that means the growing suburbs that encircle the big cities. "We have tremendously large numbers of unskilled workers settling on the outskirts," says Lawrence. "There are huge influxes in places like Long Island. . . . These sorts of sweeping patterns are going unnoticed."

Beyond that, it's very hard to generalize; South American immigrants are an extremely diverse group, with company executives and migrant farm workers, scientific geniuses and fashion models, playboy millionaires and sweatshop laborers, artists and machinists . . . the list goes on. The same thing could be said for Mexicans and Central Americans.

"I think it's important not to overdo the theme that South Americans are 'wealthy and educated' compared to the Mexicans/Central Americans who are 'poor and illiterate,'" says Lawrence. While statistically that's more likely to be true, there are many examples of the opposite trend.

"Especially at the highest income levels, and for specific South American groups in some markets, it is hardly true at all," Lawrence notes. "Venezuelans and Chileans and Argentinians are one class; Colombians and Peruvians, who are the most numerous South Americans, are quite another."

That said, South American immigrants in general tend to be more highly educated than other Latinos: 48 percent of South Americans in the United States have gone to college, compared with 14 percent of Mexicans, 23 percent of Central Americans, and 38 percent of Caribbean islanders, according to U.S. Census Bureau data. The rate for immigrants overall is 42 percent; for U.S. natives, 52 percent.

As one would expect, a college education pays off for South American immigrants in the form of better job opportunities. About 23 percent of South Americans are professionals or managers, compared with 6 percent of Mexicans, 9 percent of Central Americans, and 23 percent of Caribbean islanders. Another 24 percent of South Americans are technicians or in sales or administrative jobs, compared with 11 percent of

Mexicans, 18 percent of Central Americans, and 25 percent of Caribbean islanders (mostly Cubans).

There's an even bigger difference when one compares lower-wage workers—for example, farm workers, manual laborers, and those who are employed in the service industry, such as restaurant and hotel workers. Just over half of South Americans fall into that category, compared with 83 percent of Mexicans and 73 percent of Central Americans. Caribbean islanders are more comparable to South Americans, with only 52 percent in manual, farm, and service jobs.

The available statistics for Canada's South American population aren't nearly as detailed. Compared with the United States, a much larger country, Canada attracts relatively few immigrants from South America. The nation's 2011 census counted about 380,000 South American immigrants, of whom more than 42 percent came from Guyana. About 8 in 10 Guyanese Canadians live in Toronto.

Colombian Americans

Like many immigrant groups, Colombian Americans have distinguished themselves in the professional and business worlds. Early immigrants from Colombia were not fleeing war or persecution; they arrived as middle-class professionals, established themselves in New York and Florida, and built a strong base from there. Many Colombians are concentrated with other Andean immigrants—mainly Peruvians and Ecuadorians—in the Roosevelt Avenue area of Queens. In the Miami area, they vie with Cubans for influence and power.

Others, like Hurtado, followed their hearts to the heartland.

Hurtado met his future wife, Julia, when she was working in the Peace Corps in his native town of Popayán. They fell in love, married, and had children. Although violence was common in the countryside, in Bogotá, where they lived, life was good.

But Julia's parents were growing older, and the couple felt it was time to take their children to the United States, where they could learn English and take advantage of the greater economic

Immigrants to the United States send a total of almost $50 billion a year in remittances to their relatives in their home countries.

opportunities. They settled in Missouri, where Julia was born and where her parents still lived. They made their homes there and raised three children.

Second-generation Colombians, like the children of immigrants from other nations, have gained from their parents' decision to move to North America. Hurtado's daughter Sandra followed in her father's footsteps, working as an accountant in state government. By 2003 she was the second-highest official in Missouri's planning and budget office.

Of the approximately 707,000 Colombians counted by the 2010 U.S. census, about 200,000 were living in New York City, which boasted the nation's largest Colombian community. The trend began in the 1940s when several hundred white, middle-class Colombians moved to New York and settled in the Jackson Heights neighborhood of Queens. Since that time, thousands of Colombians have migrated to the area, which is now more racially diverse and includes Afro-Colombians and mestizos as well as the white, middle-class group.

Colombians in New York have created several support groups. The grandfather of them all is the Centro Cívico Colombiano, founded in 1980 to give Colombians a place to meet and gather. For years the Centro provided English classes and other services. In 2000, when Humberto Orjuela became president, the group launched an ambitious educational and social program that includes classes in English and Spanish, citizenship, computing, folkloric dancing, yoga, and nutrition. For those who never completed their education, the Centro offers classes to help people pass the high school graduate equivalency exam. And the programs are open to everyone—not just Colombians—so the Colombians are taking a lead in organizing and educating the entire immigrant community. The group also has taken the lead in promoting an enormously popular Colombian Independence Day celebration in New York City.

In Miami the Colombian American Service Association (CASA), established in 1994, has developed a strong presence. The 2010 census put the Colombian community in Florida at about 175,000, but CASA and other groups estimate that the actually number of Colombians in Miami alone is close to 300,000, if those who are there illegally are taken into account.

Colombian communities are also thriving in New Jersey, Boston, Houston, Atlanta, Chicago, and California, among other locales.

Peruvian and Ecuadorian Americans

Immigrants to the United States from the Andean nations of Peru and Ecuador have made their mark on both coasts. Peruvians constitute the largest South American group in California, with numbers estimated at 65,000 in 2010. They are concentrated in the Los Angeles and San Francisco areas, particularly around San Mateo. The San Francisco area boasts eight different Peruvian clubs, according to Stanford University professor José Carlos Fajardo. Los Angeles has its own Peruvian Chamber of Commerce, and there's even a Peruvian-Japanese organization there.

But more Peruvians make their home in the New York–New Jersey area than anywhere else in the United States—an estimated 100,000 individuals in 2010. Strong Peruvian communities also flourish in Miami (almost 54,000) and the Washington, D.C., area (about 23,000).

Ecuadorian immigrants have flocked to the Big Apple: nearly two-thirds of the more than 424,000 Ecuadorians counted by the 2010 U.S. census live in the New York metropolitan area. Many work in construction jobs. In addition, the New York area is home to a number of Ecuadorian jewelers, most of whom arrived about a decade ago. Janet Tapia of the *Ecuador News* explains that, because of their country's rich gold mines, the tradition of working in gold has been passed down from one generation of Ecuadorians to the next.

Outside of New York, other important Ecuadorian communities exist in Florida, home to almost 30,000 Ecuadorians in 2000; California, home to about 22,000; and Chicago, home to about 12,000.

Guyanese Americans

Some people believe that the number of Guyanese living abroad may exceed the number living in Guyana itself. In Canada alone, the Guyanese community equals about 12 percent of Guyana's total population. In the United States, the Guayanese community totals about 273,000.

The Guyanese are quite different culturally from other South American groups—in part because they speak English, and in part because half of them are of East Indian descent. In New York City, a special place for English-speaking Caribbean islanders such as Jamaicans and Trinidadians, the Guyanese have prospered. As small-business owners they have created their own wealth, rebuilding run-down inner-city areas from the ground up.

Outside of New York, the Guyanese communities in the United States are relatively small. The 2010 census recorded an estimated 18,000 Guyanese in Florida, but only 5,000 in

California, and fewer than 1,500 in Chicago.

Brazilian Americans

The majority of Brazilian immigrants to the United States come from the enormous central state of Minas Gerais—and the most prominent "sender" city, Governador Valadares, was the former home of at least 15,000 Brazilians living in the Massachusetts towns of Framingham and Marlborough.

Other sizable Brazilian communities in the United States are found in New York City; Newark, New Jersey; and Pompano Beach, Florida. According to the Brazilian consulate in New York, there are more than 150,000 *brazucas* living in New York, New Jersey, Connecticut, Delaware, and Pennsylvania, the areas covered by that department.

A study by the New York City government found that of the 2,761 Brazilians who had received their green card in the city between 1995 and 1996, a total of 27 percent were living in the Upper East Side, a pricey area where apartments rent for $5,000 a month, according to the newsmagazine *Brazzil*.

New York's Brazilian community is impressive in its size and its prosperity, but it's not as tightly knit or as highly concentrated as the Brazilian communities in Massachusetts, according to Joel Millman, in his book *The Other Americans*. "Just as Governador Valadares may be the southernmost part of the United States, Framingham is becoming the northernmost town in Brazil," he writes.

Immigrants from Argentina, Uruguay, and Chile

Compared with other Latino groups, people from the Southern Cone nations Argentina, Chile, and Uruguay have a rather low profile in the United States. In part this is because their numbers are relatively small: the 2000 U.S. census counted just over 100,000 Argentines (which was not enough to rank among the top 10 Latino groups), fewer than 69,000 Chileans, and fewer than 19,000 Uruguayans. But in part the lower profile is due to the greater ease with which people from southern South America *assimilate* into North American culture. They have not formed many extensive communities of their own *paisanos* in North America but have instead gravitated more toward the mainstream of U.S. and Canadian society.

"We have been the luckiest," said Argentine economist Luis Brunstein. "We tend to be accepted based on our looks; we look more European . . . intuitively, we tend to do better financially."

That doesn't mean it's necessarily easy for them, however. Brunstein reflects on the culture clash for Southern Cone natives:

> Argentines tend to have the culture from the old Europe, the customs of the Spaniards and the French and the English. Our values are not as pragmatic or materialistic as people in the United States. We tend to be more socially oriented; we need a network of people around us, to be part of a community.
>
> Here the first thing you see right away is a sense of isolation, a lack of true friendship. Here friendship is a difficult concept. You're not going to be finding many people will be truly your friend. There, people want to be in groups and spend more time socializing; here, people are not all that interested in you.
>
> People from Argentina always arrive at the same conclusion: This is a great country for us to work. But this is not a country where you want to retire.

So the dream to return is deferred to retirement. And then, with the children settled and married, and with grandchildren and friends and extended family, it becomes harder still to leave.

 # Text-Dependent Questions

1. In what areas—large cities or rural regions—do most South American immigrants live in the United States?
2. What is the size of the Guayanese community in the United States?

 # Research Project

Immigration reform has long been a controversial issue in American politics. Investigate the positions of leading Democrats and leading Republicans. Which side do you agree with? Do you think both sides have valid points? Write a one-page essay on what you think the United States should do about its current immigration system. Remember to support your opinions by citing relevant evidence.

5 A FOOT IN EACH WORLD

Twenty-six years after he left Argentina, Eduardo Crespi doesn't think too much about his homeland. "There are more interesting things going on here," he said. As he painted a door in his remodeled vintage farmhouse, he contemplated the question: "What do you do to maintain your connection to your heritage—and pass it on to your daughter?"

"That's a good question," he responded, standing back to admire his handiwork, and then turning to his daughter. "What do we do, Nicole?"

Nicole is eight years old and has inherited her father's brown eyes and her mother's red hair. Born of an Argentine and a Missourian, she looks more the part of a happy Midwesterner. But when she switches to Spanish mode, she is 100 percent Latina.

"We speak Spanish," she answers quickly. And as she thinks about what it means to be Argentine, she draws a blank. Then she remembers. "Pictures," she says. "We like to look at pictures."

Someday she hopes to go to Argentina for a visit, perhaps even to study at the University of Buenos Aires. But for now, her life is based in a farmhouse in central Missouri, and the horses

◀ The *quinceañera*—an often lavish party marking a girl's 15th birthday—is a tradition South American immigrants to the United States and Canada have kept alive.

that graze outside her bedroom window are the closest she'll get to the pampas for a long time.

Fitting in and Staying Connected

Most South Americans from the Southern Cone countries—Argentines, Uruguayans, and Chileans—have integrated so well into the fabric of North American society that the only thing that differentiates them from the crowd is their accent. Because the Southern Cone was heavily settled by Europeans—first Spaniards, then Italians, then Germans—and because not much of the indigenous population remains, people from these countries tend to be culturally more like North Americans.

This is true, to some extent, for immigrants from most South American countries. That's because it tends to be the wealthier classes who have the resources to emigrate, and the wealthier classes from all Latin American countries tend to be the descendants of white Europeans.

But a growing number of South Americans living in North America claim indigenous and African roots. Some put their heritage aside and work very hard to live in the mainstream of North American society. Others hold fast to their roots, seeing their heritage as an essential part of who they are.

For many Argentines and Uruguayans, links to the past are in simple things—like passing a maté cup and chatting, or hosting a big barbecue. An Argentine barbecue, in particular, can be a large and expensive affair, with massive quantities of the best beef in three or four different cuts, roasted slowly over the fire as old friends reminisce about old times, and newcomers are

 Words to Understand in This Chapter

diaspora—the community of people of the same nationality living outside their homeland.

lingua franca—a language that is adopted as a common language between speakers whose native languages are different.

brought into the fold.

Other groups, like the people of Peru, Colombia, and Ecuador, tend to be more deeply connected to their indigenous heritage. Many cities have active Peruvian, Colombian, and Ecuadorian societies that celebrate regional traditions with festivals, folkloric dance presentations, and native costumes.

The Colombian Independence Day celebration in New York City on July 20 is just one example. In 2015 the festival drew an estimated 800,000 people. There were booths from dozens of countries, from Argentina to Ecuador, and the aromas of a dozen cuisines filled the air as people wandered from spectacle to spectacle, listening to the haunting pan pipes, the merry and raucous drumming of the Afro-Latino sound, and the toe-tapping rhythms of Caribbean salsa and merengue.

The event was such a phenomenal success, according to organizer Humberto Orjuela, because of its multicultural nature. The Colombians have taken the lead in New York City in giving all Latinos a forum to celebrate their heritage.

Brazilians in New York join the fun on July 20. But they also celebrate their own independence from Portugal on September 7. The Brazilian Street Festival takes place in "Little Brazil," the area of Manhattan's 46th Street known for its concentration of Brazilian business and social establishments. The event is co-sponsored by the Brazilian American Cultural Center and the *Brasilians*, a flourishing national bilingual newspaper serving the Brazilian community throughout the United States.

The Ecuadorian independence celebration on August 10 features a parade down 37th Avenue in Queens, with thematic floats, folkloric dances, and performers of all kinds. The festivities end with an arts festival in Flushing Park, where Ecuadorian artisans display their handiwork, Ecuadorian restaurants delight the palate, and Ecuadorian businesses distribute publicity about their wares. "It's bigger than Christmas," says Janet Tapia of the *Ecuador News*.

Peruvians in Patterson, New Jersey, hold one of the world's largest religious processions every October. The procession is in

honor of El Señor de los Milagros (Christ of the Miracles).

And it's been the same in other parts of the country—Mexicans in the West, Peruvians in the Midwest, Colombians in Florida, and Brazilians in Massachusetts have worked hard to liberate the colorful and dynamic traditions of their fellow Latinos. South Americans have taken the lead in organizing cultural festivals such as Hispanic Heritage Month. Such events have been gaining in popularity with the rise of a new sense of multiculturalism. Black, Latino, and Asian community leaders have been more vocal about their pride, and people have felt freer to share—and even celebrate—their differences.

A Pan-Latino Culture?

Another phenomenon that has emerged from all of this is a flourishing new Hispanic culture that crosses old dividing lines

New York City's 46th Street comes alive with the sights, sounds, and tastes of Brazil on September 7. That's when Brazilians—and a host of others who love their vibrant, expressive culture—mark Brazil's independence from Portugal with a joyous street festival.

and national borders. "The talk of a pan-Latino culture is fairly recent," says essayist Ilan Stavans, author of *The Hispanic Condition* and *Spanglish: The Making of a New American Language*:

> Hispanics north of the Rio Grande trace their roots to the colonial period, but the rapid growth of the community took place in the twentieth century and is the result of immigration. People from every corner of the Americas have sought El Norte as an alternative way of life. And their arrival has forced them to interact with Spanish speakers with whom they never interacted before. Thus, the Southwest is the habitat of Mexicans, Guatemalans, Salvadorans, etc. Likewise, New York is a melting pot where Dominicans, Puerto Ricans, Cubans, Colombians and other south-of-the-border immigrants find themselves tete-a-tete.

Several factors have combined to spur unity among Hispanics: the rapid demographic growth of the Latino population; the explosion of the ethnic media, led by Telemundo and Univision; and, as Stavans puts it, the "middle-classization" of a new generation of Latinos.

"It has to do," Stavans says, "with erasing borders within the Latino community: 'Yes, I was a Puerto Rican, you were an Argentine—but guess what? Now we're all Latino. Or are we not?' There is a sum of parts that is greater than the whole. We are creating a culture that is different from the one our parents had."

Indeed, it's a culture with its own language: Spanglish, long denigrated by the older generation as a messy abomination, is now becoming the **lingua franca** of the young Latino set. "Nothing is as distinctive and unique," says Stavans, who is responsible for a translation of the early sections of *Don Quixote of La Mancha* into Spanglish. "Spanglish is more than simply a language, it's a state of mind."

Stavans teamed up with cartoonist Lalo Alcaraz in a fun-to-read cartoon celebration of Spanglish in *Latino USA: A Cartoon History*. And Alcaraz proclaims in his website, pocho.com, "Spanglish is our Language!" (*Pocho* is a word for acculturated Mexicans in the United States.)

Speaking Two Languages

Spanish teacher Nancy Malugani has already raised three children, and all she can do now is nag at her youngest two to practice their Spanish. Ernesto, the oldest, was nine years old when they left the seaside city of Montevideo, Uruguay, so he remembers. But Pablo and Laura, raised in suburbia on a diet of MTV and Coca-Cola, have little connection with Uruguay.

"Honestly, I don't think I did a very good job of it," said Malugani. "I tried to remind them of their heritage when I first came here, but the kids separated themselves from that because they wanted to belong. It wasn't till they became adolescents that they came up with this 'I am Latino' thing.

"But I keep my own life, which is very much my own. Deep inside I feel very much a Latin but I've assimilated the American culture."

She's an excellent cook of Uruguayan cuisine—which looks very much like Italian. Like many Uruguayans, Malugani is of Italian heritage. Her friendships and her connections with Uruguay are constant; friends and professional contacts from back home still come to visit, 20 years after her departure. For all her assimilation, she's still very Uruguayan. But sometimes she's disappointed that her children are not.

If she had it to do over again? "I would have enforced speaking in Spanish all the time in the house," she says. "It's sad, because they've lost a tool that would be good for them professionally. But more important, they lost the opportunity of communicating with their own family."

South Americans raising their children nowadays are more aware of the need to retain their heritage. José and Janette García, a professional Bolivian couple who have lived in the United States for close to a decade, are raising their two daughters in a multicultural world. Janette is part of an outreach effort by the Girl Scouts, building up Latina Girl Scout troops throughout the Midwest.

Like other immigrant parents, they perform a tricky balancing act—helping their children succeed in an English-language

Networking for the People

Many South Americans are playing an important role in helping their fellow Latinos find their way in North America. Argentines, Colombians, Uruguayans, and Peruvians have all reached out a hand to fellow Spanish speakers in need. Some have volunteered as translators and guides, helping the newcomers negotiate the difficult system in their adopted country. Others have taken jobs in social work and health care so they could provide badly needed services in the comforting language of home. Some, like Eduardo Crespi, have done all of the above.

Crespi left his native Argentina during the violence of the late 1970s as a 17-year-old hitchhiker. Many of his friends were "disappeared" by the dictatorial regime, and he took off across Latin America and then Europe on an international adventure that lasted more than a decade.

He met Barbara Brockman, the Missouri woman who was to become his wife, while he was working as a tour guide in Cuzco, Peru. They made their way to the United States, where Crespi took on a variety of jobs, from roofer to telemarketer to factory worker. Then he followed the path of many new immigrants: He started his own business on a shoestring—several businesses, actually, beginning with house painting and ending with a restaurant. Meanwhile, he was going to school at night to follow another longtime dream: working in the health care field. He decided he was too old to become a doctor, so he studied nursing.

When rising numbers of Latino workers began to show up in the Midwest to meet the growing demand for labor, Crespi was among the first to notice the trend. He soon began to see that nobody was meeting the needs of the majority of these newcomers.

So in April of 2000, with the help of Brockman, now a bilingual therapist, and a handful of volunteers, he launched the Centro Latino in Columbia, Missouri. The project pulled together all his skills—as an entrepreneur, as a nurse, and now as a community organizer—to ease the transition of the wave of newcomers. Most of all, he drew on the skills that he'd learned as a constantly moving immigrant: "how to get a working visa, how to get money, how to create something from nothing. . . . That's why I understand the immigrants I work with."

Today the Centro is bustling with activity. It's funded through several grants and has a staff of 30 volunteers and a variety of programs. It moved into a larger building in 2011. Besides the clinic, staffed by Crespi and another health care worker, it offers classes in English and Spanish, computers and citizenship, yoga and martial arts. There are after-school sessions for the children, and field trips for the families to cultural and educational sites around the state. The center is open for referrals, classes, and health care services six days a week. And his model is being duplicated by Latino groups around the state.

"It's network marketing for the good of the people," he jokes.

The first lesson for his many clients is to follow his example. "We can do things without any money, and that's what we were doing," Crespi says. "If we get money, great; we can have sugar in the coffee. We can have a great life with just a little bit."

culture while at the same time retaining their Spanish skills and sense of heritage. And they both devote considerable thought to the best ways to teach Esteli, seven, and Violeta, two, about their heritage and their mother tongue.

José, who worked with migrant farm workers and other Latino groups for about five years, used to worry that Esteli would grow up speaking with an accent and perhaps be at a disadvantage or even be discriminated against. He didn't want her to fall behind in school, have trouble making friends, or be treated differently just because of her accent, so he worked hard on her English skills.

Now the tables have turned. What Daddy does is still important for Esteli, but her life is now divided between two worlds: one is her Bolivian family, and the other is the public school she attends. It's becoming important to fit in with the crowd, to be like the other girls. When her father speaks to her in Spanish, she answers him in English.

"I just don't listen," says José. "I say, '*No te entiendo* (I don't understand).' She says, 'Yes, you do,' and she keeps talking. I just ignore her until she starts speaking Spanish."

Janette worries about Esteli losing her Spanish, too. She began to feel her daughter pulling away as she approached school age.

"I started to feel it when she was four years old—then she said to me one day, 'I don't want to speak any more Spanish. It's awful,' " Janette recalls.

"I said, 'No it's not, it's cool—and you're going to see why it's cool.' "

Janette, who lived in Minneapolis, took her daughter to a volunteer interpreting assignment with a clinic for pregnant Latina women. A clinic worker named Mary spoke no Spanish, while most of the women spoke no English.

"Why don't you ask them what they would like to drink?" Janette prompted her daughter as they approached the patients.

"*¿Qué quieres tomar?*" the little one asked the ladies.

"*Jugo de manzana,*" one of them responded gratefully, as

Mary looked on, not knowing that the request was for apple juice.

"You see, Esteli—poor Mary, she cannot understand what these women are saying. And these poor women cannot understand Mary. But you can understand both of them!"

From that day on, Janette says, Esteli never again said that she didn't want to speak Spanish. And since that time, she's become something of a trendsetter at her elementary school. Several classmates were inspired by her example and asked their parents to let them take Spanish classes. When her father came to school in his poncho to play his collection of Bolivian flutes, Esteli was suddenly all the rage. She was dressed in her embroidered shawl and *pollera* (an Andean-style skirt), and they gave a presentation to the class.

"Esteli was particularly excited," says José. "She felt very proud of being Bolivian."

Melting Pot or Salad Bowl?

For South Americans, it's important to recognize that not all Latinos want to fit into one multicultural stew. "I don't like the idea of the melting pot," says Chilean author Isabel Allende. "I like the idea of the salad bowl, in which every ingredient makes the salad better. Each ingredient adds to the salad's flavors, and it wouldn't be what it is without every ingredient."

That's true for Latinos as a whole, and it's also true for people from different subcultures within each country. José Carlos Fajardo, a Peruvian from the Andean highlands city of Ayacucho, says it's important not to lump all Peruvians together, for example. He cites the Peruvian festival for El Señor de los Milagros, which is celebrated in Lima and throughout the Peruvian *diaspora*.

But for all the joy that El Señor de los Milagros brings to *Limeños*, he means little to *Ayacuchanos*, who celebrate a different representation of Christ—or to the people of Cuzco, who celebrate yet another one. They might attend a Milagros celebration out of a sense of solidarity with fellow Peruvians, but it's no substitute for their own celebration. And there are many Quechua people from the Andes who aren't Catholic, Fajardo notes. "So the Christ and the Virgin are not important for them," he says. "What's more important than Christ is the Pachamama, the Mother Earth."

Rather than associating primarily with their countrymen and women, some South American immigrants in North America find themselves gravitating toward people from other groups who share similar interests and values. Peruvian Daniel Juarez, for example, became involved with the Peruvian Society when he first came to St. Louis. But he soon lost interest in the focus on social events and fund-raisers to benefit people back home; Juarez was more compelled to work with incoming immigrants who were in need of assistance. "[The Peruvian Society] always had a way to participate, and that's fine—it just wasn't the kind of participation I wanted to do," he said.

Although it's starting to change in the United States, South Americans—and, indeed, Latin Americans in general—have traditionally socialized with their own kind: Peruvians with Peruvians, Colombians with Colombians, and so forth, celebrating their own holidays and their own traditions. An Argentine is quick to distinguish himself from a Mexican, and vice versa. But a growing Latino identity is beginning to cross those distinctive cultural lines, and a sense of Latino pride is getting stronger. It can be seen at Hispanic Heritage Month celebrations, in which people come to watch folkloric dances and hear music from all over the Americas—and to marvel at the vast diversity of Latin American culture.

Staying in Touch

The advent of international calling cards makes it much easier for South American immigrants to call home to talk to *Mamá* or *los niños*. With rates sometimes as low as 5 cents a minute, an immigrant can telephonically drop in on a birthday celebration or visit an ailing relative in the hospital thousands of miles away.

Radio stations in Colombia have dedicated programs to the

Univision, one of two major Spanish-language television networks in the United States, has fostered a growing Latino identity.

call-in voices of loved ones abroad. But one technology has helped pull people together across the miles more than any other. The Internet has enabled growing numbers of Latinos to stay in touch with their far-flung relatives—at least for those who have access to a computer. Groups of *paisanos* from particular countries—Peruvians, Colombians, Venczuelans, and Argentines, to name a few—are compiling large e-mail lists and notifying one another of items of interest, sending missives that make their way to the diaspora around the world in seconds.

Electronic versions of South American newspapers have also become popular, as people log on to their favorite daily's website to stay abreast of the latest news. But more than a source for news, the papers have become a forum for those living abroad, and a way to stay in touch.

El Universo of Ecuador is leading the way, with a space on its website dedicated to publishing brief messages from

A family from South America celebrates receiving Canadian citizenship.

Ecuadorians abroad. Every day the site features 25 pages, each containing 20 personal messages, which come from nearly every U.S. state and from all over Europe and Asia.

A burgeoning Internet culture has also proved fertile ground for specialized Web publications, such as the Peruvian magazine *Ciberayllu* (meaning something akin to "Cyber-village" in a sort of Spanglish-Quechua blend). The magazine was the brainchild of Domingo Martínez Castilla, a Peruvian agro-economist who came to the United States in 1986. He began the project in 1996 as a way of staying in touch with the literary culture of his homeland. Soon it surpassed his expectations in popularity as a showcase for the global Peruvian community and a gathering place for lovers of Latin American literature worldwide. He receives submissions from more than 25 countries, while more than a thousand surfers visit the site daily. It's purely a labor of love, as after seven years it's still a volunteer vocation.

"Those of us who migrated because we wanted to or even if we didn't want to are our country's investments," he told *Adelante* reporter Sara Fajardo, a fellow Peruvian. "We received an education there, and it is unjust that we leave and forget our homeland. This is my payment. It's minor. I pay little for all I've been given."

But the developing Pan-Latino culture has flourished on the Internet as well, crossing lines of class and nationality. Local, regional, and national networks have sprung up on subjects as varied as immigration reform, civil rights, and health care for Latinos. When *Vanity Fair* ran a satirical column by its fictional columnist Dame Edna, deriding Spanish as the language of the hired help, e-mail networks were aflame for weeks afterward with the discussions. *Vanity Fair* was eventually forced to publish an apology. As the *Los Angeles Times* joked, "Ticking off a bunch of Latinos with laptops can be a dangerous thing."

 Text-Dependent Questions

1. On what date is the Colombian Independence Day celebration held in New York City?
2. What are some factors that have combined to spur unity among Hispanics in the United States?

 Research Project

If you are of South American heritage, write about how your family celebrates a traditional holiday or festival, or about a specific celebration that was particularly memorable for you. If you aren't of South American heritage, research a traditional holiday or festival (such as the Carnival in Rio de Janeiro, Brazil, or Inti Raymi in Cuzco, Peru) and write a one-page report.

6 PROBLEMS FACING SOUTH AMERICANS IN NORTH AMERICA

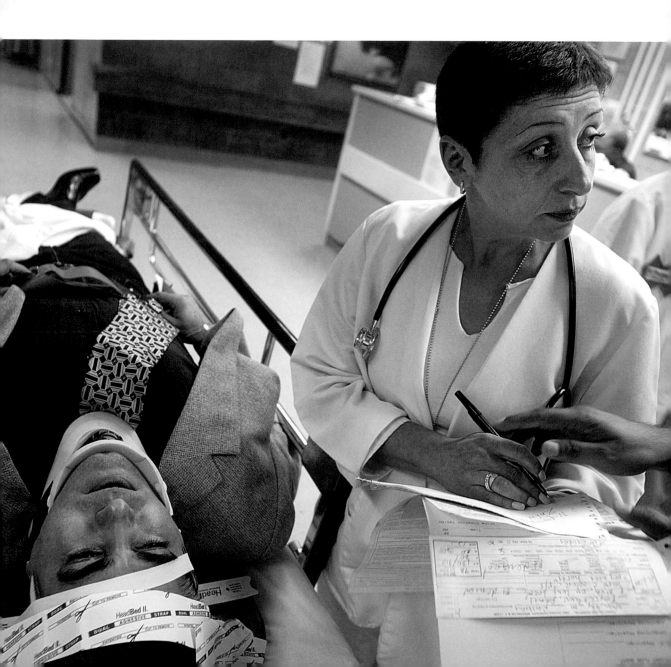

Like any other immigrant group, South Americans come to the United States clutching their version of the American Dream. In their search for a better life in *El Norte*, they have faced many of the same barriers as other Latino immigrants (and other immigrants in general). But some of the difficulties South Americans have encountered are unique. Chief among these difficulties is being confused for something they're not. In the United States and Canada, South Americans will probably always be a minority within a minority, and for many, establishing an identity separate from the larger Hispanic community is an important, if difficult, priority.

Like all new immigrants coming from non-English-speaking countries, South Americans have had to struggle to overcome the language barrier. And though they might achieve competence, that's not the same as blending in. For those who were older when they arrived, their accent may always cause them difficulties. For Brazilians and for those who speak indigenous languages, such as the Quechua-speaking people of the Andes, the adjustment has been particularly difficult, since many of the programs designed to help Latinos are geared to Spanish speakers.

Immigrants from all over the world, like the working poor who are U.S. citizens, have struggled with health care concerns,

◀ For Latino immigrants with limited English skills, communicating with health care providers during a medical emergency can be a potentially life-threatening problem. Health insurance is also a major concern among Latinos—as many as half of whom may be uninsured, according to a recent survey.

particularly when they are uninsured. For Hispanics with limited English-language skills, finding an interpreter in times of a health care emergency can be difficult. Even for those who speak English, getting access to medical insurance can be a problem. According to the American College of Emergency Physicians, 30 percent of all uninsured people in the United States in 2012 were Hispanic. By comparison, the rate for African Americans was 20 percent; for whites, 15 percent. That means there were nearly 15 million uninsured Hispanics living in the United States.

For immigrants and refugees fleeing war, natural disasters, or economic crises, financial difficulties are almost a given. Making matters worse is that some immigrants are victims of fraud. Across the country, immigrant advocates warn their clients about an astounding variety of con artists, who prey on the vulnerable newcomers with high-priced and *fraudulent* "immigration services," pyramid schemes, and other scams.

Discrimination and Stereotypes

South Americans in the United States have reported a variety of experiences with discrimination. In an August 2015 survey conducted by the Gallup Organization, about one in four Hispanic respondants reported being discriminated against during the previous month. Places where the discrimination occurred included their place of work, in dealings with police, while getting healthcare, at entertainment venues such as bars or restaurants, and while while shopping in stores.

Gallup found that Hispanics born outside of the country were much more likely than those born in the U.S. to say they

 Words to Understand in This Chapter

fraudulent—wrongful or criminal deception intended to result in financial or personal gain.
paternalistic—behavior by an organization or state which limits some person or group's liberty or autonomy for what is presumed to be that person's or group's own good.

Demonstrators protest for immigration reform in Los Angeles, 2015.

had experienced discrimination in the past month. For example, while 18 percent of foreign-born Hispanics said they were treated unfairly at their place of work because of their ethnicity, only 5 percent of U.S.-born Hispanics reported experiencing workplace discrimination.

Foreign-born Hispanics (15 percent) were five times more likely than U.S.-born Hispanics (3 percent) to say they experienced discrimination because they are Hispanic while getting healthcare for themselves or for a family member.

A National Survey of Latinos revealed discrimination of another sort, well known among Latinos but less so among non-Latinos: Hispanics discriminating against other Hispanics. A staggering 83 percent of respondents identified this as a problem in this 2002 study, and almost half (47 percent) considered it a major problem. Respondents most often attributed this discrimination to differences in education or income levels (more-educated members of the upper or middle class discriminating against members of the working class, for instance). But, as the survey report noted, "a substantial number also feel that Latinos discriminate against other Latinos because they or their parents or ancestors are from a different country of origin."

One Argentine living in California reported that some Mexican Americans there would not speak to her in Spanish. She also said she was denied a job in Spanish-language radio because of her Argentine accent.

In the view of some observers, the media perpetuate inaccurate stereotypes about Hispanics. "The media has a certain filter when they report about Latinos," says Stewart Lawrence, an immigration analyst in Washington, D.C. "There's a composite about the poor, urban, barrio-dwelling Latino that's stereotypical."

Another stereotype comes in the guise of charity—a paternalistic attitude toward the newcomers that stifles their adaptation in their new community. Celia Organista, a Hispanic advocate in Watsonville, California, calls it "the *pobrecito* syndrome," after the Spanish word meaning "poor little thing." It's the tendency to assume that "they" need help, and "we" know what's best for them.

"These are people with good hearts, but they have a **paternalistic** approach: Let me help you," said Eduardo Crespi, the community organizer from Argentina. "It's nice for awhile; it makes the [immigrants] feel protected. But what happens when they go away?"

Displaced Professionals

For some highly educated South Americans, coming to the United States presents a professional dilemma. That's because the licensing requirements for certain professions don't allow the transfer of a license from a Latin American country. Thus an immigrant wishing to continue a career as a physician, dentist, veterinarian, nurse, or lawyer might have to go through years of expensive and time-consuming retraining. For a doctor, passing

Pablo's Story

Pablo Ureta was like a lot of American teenagers. He went to a regular high school and hung out with regular guys. He liked to party. He knew how to make others laugh and have a good time. In one way, however, Pablo was different. He wasn't born in the United States; he was born in Montevideo, Uruguay, and came to the United States when he was eight years old.

At the age of 19, he followed the bad advice of a friend and got in on a drug deal. It was a decision that would cost him more than he could have ever imagined. That's because for Pablo Ureta, a non-citizen of the United States, the rules were about to change.

More than three years after the drug deal, following a lengthy investigation and court proceeding, Pablo was persuaded to plead guilty to conspiracy. By this time, he had settled down: he had gotten a good job installing telecommunications equipment and had married his high school sweetheart, and the couple had a baby on the way. Wilson Ureta—named after Pablo's deceased father—was born while Pablo was serving his year-and-a-half sentence in a federal prison.

In the spring of 2001, having done his time, Pablo was released. The future seemed full of promise. He settled into the role of husband and father and returned to his old job. He made plans to become a U.S. citizen and go back to school to improve his skills.

On May 24, 2002, Pablo took what he thought would be a routine trip to the local office of the Immigration and Naturalization Service to get his expired work permit renewed. To his shock, he was immediately sent to jail. The agency's computers had flagged him as a criminal who must be deported.

Federal legislation had been passed that would require automatic deportation for legal immigrants who had committed an "aggravated felony," which includes most drug-related crimes. The law was retroactive, meaning that even people who had committed their crimes before the legislation was passed—people like Pablo, who had broken the law years before, as a teenager—would be affected. Such people would have no options.

Since the passage, in 1996, of the Illegal Immigration Reform and Immigrant Responsibility Act, judges could no longer consider the facts of an individual's case and grant relief if the judge believed the person had changed his or her ways and met other criteria. Thousands of immigrants have reportedly been jailed and deported under the law—many of them, critics say, for relatively minor offenses.

While Pablo languished in jail—under the law, many immigrants awaiting the resolution of their cases are ineligible for release on bond—his family scoured the country to find a lawyer willing to take the case; most said it was hopeless. By 2003, he had exhausted all his appeals and was deported back to a country he barely remembered, with no friends or family that he knew, with no memory of the Spanish language. Uruguay, in the midst of an economic crisis at the time, had little to offer a young man like Pablo Ureta.

Many Hispanic immigrants, such as these Peruvian men, find work in restaurants.

the U.S. licensure requirements may take six years. Many choose to start new careers.

"I know quite a few doctors working in restaurants," says Humberto Orjuela. "There are a lot of displaced professionals here. Many of them are studying on the side and trying to progress. Sometimes it takes years—they do it a little at a time, while they are working and supporting their families."

Diana Mesa, volunteer coordinator at the Colombian American Service Association in Miami, observed the same trend. "We have a massive flood of professionals, doctors, lawyers and so on," Mesa said.

Spanish teacher Nancy Malugani is one example. A veterinarian from Uruguay, she came to the United States on a United Nations fellowship in 1984. She met and married a U.S. citizen and decided to stay. Rather than repeating all her schooling, she decided to start a new career as a junior high and university teacher.

"It would have cost me a lot of money and a lot of years of work," she said. "I wanted to do something different. I love kids, so I decided to be a teacher."

Malugani has won national recognition for her lively and creative approach to teaching. Over the years, she has also used her position as a teacher to do outreach with students having trouble, serving as an interpreter and a link between Spanish-speaking parents and the school system.

But Malugani wanted to do more. When a rapid influx of Spanish-speaking immigrants began coming to Missouri in the 1990s, she became a volunteer translator and a counselor to people in need. She also helped found a bilingual newspaper for Latinos called *Adelante*.

"It's natural to want to help 'your own' people," she says. "There is always a special bond between Latinos, and one feels a moral responsibility to help each other." Like many Latinos who volunteer to help the newcomers, she considers her community work a natural response to people in need—"not a big deal."

"I think I'm just giving back something I've received all my life," she says. "I've been lucky all my life and have received help when I needed it. But you never know when the coin is going to turn around. . . . It's just something you do because you want the whole world to be better."

 ## Text-Dependent Questions

1. What percentage of uninsured people in the United States were Hispanic in 2012?
2. Where are five areas that Hispanics reported being discriminated against in 2015?

 ## Research Project

To become a U.S. citizen, an immigrant from another country must pass a civics test. U.S. Citizenship and Immigration Services offers practice tests at: https://my.uscis.gov/prep/test/civics/view

Take a test. What percentage did you get correct? Do some further research about any answers you got wrong.

7 THE FUTURE OF SOUTH AMERICANS IN NORTH AMERICA

Over the past fifty years, the United States (and, to a lesser degree, Canada) has seen a dramatic increase in immigration from South America. Will that trend continue? The answer may depend as much on conditions inside the countries of South America as on U.S. immigration policy. People who face bleak prospects in their homeland have strong motivations to go where conditions are better. Furthermore, while the United States can regulate the number of legal immigrants it accepts annually, sealing the borders to those who would enter illegally is quite another matter. Thus, in the absence of significant economic improvements in many South American countries, it is likely that each year many thousands will come to the United States any way they can.

Positive Signs

Regardless of future immigration trends, there is no doubt that South Americans have established themselves as a vital part of the largest minority group in the United States, Hispanics. And Hispanics have made their way into the mainstream of American society, culturally, and economically.

◀ With more than 3 million people of South American descent already living in the United States, and over 70,000 more arriving each year, it is clear that South American immigrants will continue to change the face of North America in the future.

"We are changing and we are being changed," observes Ilan Stavans, author of *The Hispanic Condition*. "That is very different from what happened to Latinos 20 years ago. Latinos today are finally moving from the periphery of culture to center stage.

"It used to be uncool to speak Spanish, to dance salsa or to be from the 'hood. Today these are assets. . . . Demographics have already turned the American continent upside down. Latino culture north of the Rio Grande is astonishingly alive."

The Role of Education

To get an idea of how a population is developing, and how it will look in the future, one of the most important factors is the educational level of the people, as this is something that will help determine their earning potential throughout their lives. One encouraging trend was observed by the Pew Hispanic Center in its December 2002 report, "The Improving Educational Profile of Latino Immigrants." The report examined census data from 1970 through 2000, and found that Latino immigrants were steadily gaining on their native-born counterparts in terms of education.

In 2014 the Pew Research Center released a follow-up report that found many positive signs for the South American immigrant community related to education in the United States. The report found that during the previous decade and a half, the Hispanic high school *dropout* rate had fallen dramatically. The dropout rate among Hispanics was 32 percent in 2000 among students between the ages of 18 and 24. By 2013, the rate had fallen to 14 percent among that same age group. However, Pew

 Words to Understand in This Chapter

dropout—a person who has abandoned a course of study.
multiculturalism—the co-existence of diverse cultures, where culture includes racial, religious, or cultural groups and is shown through behaviors, values, and communicative styles.

Improved access to education gives South American immigrants a better opportunity to achieve the American Dream.

noted that the Hispanic dropout rate remained higher than it was for African Americans (8 percent), whites (5 percent), or Asians (4 percent).

Pew's 2014 report also indicated that Hispanics are making big inroads in college enrollment, with the number of Hispanics enrolled in two- or four-year colleges more than tripling since 1993. In 2013, 2.2 million Hispanics were enrolled in college, up from 728,000 in 1993—a 201 percent increase. Today, Hispanics represent the largest minority group on U.S. college campuses.

Again, however, the researchers noted room for improvement. The data showed that Hispanics still lag other groups in obtaining four-year degrees. In 2013, among Hispanics ages 25 to 29, just 15 percent of Hispanics had earned a bachelor's degree or higher. By comparison, among the same age group, about 40 percent of whites, 60 percent of Asians, and 20 percent of blacks had a bachelor's degree or higher. Pew determined that this gap was partly due to the fact that Hispanics were less likely than members of other groups to enroll in a four-year college. Nearly half of the Hispanics who go on to post-secondary education attend a public two-year school, the highest share of any race or ethnicity.

One reason is that education trends over the past three decades in Latin American countries have improved considerably, as shown by the numbers of incoming immigrants who have completed primary school, high school, and college. South America continues to lead the pack, with its immigrants showing a higher education level.

Another factor is that the young Latino population is "growing up." The children of immigrants are in a better economic position than their parents, enabling them to finish high school and afford to go to college. Meanwhile, the less educated immigrant population is growing older, and the older generation is beginning to leave the labor force, making way for a younger, more educated Latino population.

In particular, the educational level of girls and women has been on the rise. In 1970 just 41 percent of the college-educated Latin American immigrants who had been educated abroad were women. By 2000 that percentage had gone up to half. Among Latinas who were educated in the United States, the trend was even more encouraging: the percentage had gone from 47 to 54 percent.

The Changing Face of Latino USA

Stavans is optimistic that the present demographic shift will be for the better, in part because of the steadily improving economic position of a maturing Latino population. "The 'middle-classization' of Latino culture is beginning to take place before our eyes," he said.

U.S. business leaders are beginning to take notice of the swelling ranks of Latinos checking out, logging on, and tuning in. Univision and Telemundo are now the nation's fastest-

Mandalit del Barco

Peru was just a collection of images in the mind of little Mandalit del Barco, growing up in Baldwin, Kansas. Those images flowered and grew in the stories of her Peruvian father and her Mexican American mother, who had met and fallen in love in the Andean city of Ayacucho.

Mandalit dreamed of faraway Peru, even writing a play for her third-grade class about an imaginary Amazon adventure. But she had been only a year old when her parents moved to Kansas, her mother's home state. Growing up, she always wanted to return and explore her roots, but violent terrorism had devastated the country in the 1980s. It was after graduate school, while she was working at her first job reporting for the *Miami Herald*, when she learned that the civil war had claimed the lives of her grandmother, her aunt, and a cousin.

So it was a decade later that she was finally able to return to her homeland. In 1999, by then a nationally known radio journalist for National Public Radio, del Barco followed in the steps of her anthropologist mother and her journalist father. She spent a year on a Fulbright scholarship in Peru, just as her mother had done in the years when she had met Mandalit's father, a newspaper reporter in Lima. Born of a long line of journalists—del Barco is a fourth-generation journalist—she passed along the passion to her younger cousin, Sara Fajardo, who accompanied and assisted her during the yearlong project. Fajardo, then an elementary school teacher, was inspired to switch to a career as a photojournalist.

But del Barco had a much different journey than her parents when she returned to the land of her birth to reclaim her Andean heritage. Her mission was to share with her Peruvian colleagues and students the radio storytelling techniques she had learned in the United States. Microphone, mini-disc recorder, and videocamera in hand, del Barco traveled all around the country recording interviews and presenting journalism workshops. As a foreign correspondent for NPR, covering the controversial political elections, she also became something of a media personality in her native land.

Del Barco preferred to focus more on the similarities than the differences. In the end, that deep connection to her Peruvian roots and her Latina heritage were what she took back home to the United States. "The whole experience made me feel even more Peruvian-Mexican American," she says.

She also came to appreciate some of the advantages of being a U.S. citizen, she says, such as freedom of the press, and multiculturalism.

Del Barco returned to her job as a reporter for National Public Radio, covering immigrant communities, the arts, and whatever strikes her fancy. As a woman thoroughly engaged in life, del Barco has a few words of advice for young people making choices about their future.

"Follow your own interests and passions, and you can make that your life's work," she advises. "I always loved writing and being in different places, being creative and adventurous. You think that when you grow up you have to be all serious and boring—it's not true. I still have a great time as a journalist, interviewing everyone from Hollywood celebrities, to gang members, to politicians—even people in the Amazon."

growing TV networks. Spanish-language publications are the fastest-growing sector of the newspaper market, as well. And major publishing houses are even launching their own Spanish-language divisions.

"It is clear that if we join forces we'll be able to get more things done," says Stavans. "It has to do with the political clout that Latinos have. Huge corporations realize we Latinos are a major source of revenue.

"Which other immigrant group has had its own major publishers? This is a major transformation."

At the same time that Latinos are becoming a more visible part of the North American landscape, a cultural globalization is taking place that is lessening the differences between Latinos and non-Latinos.

"Non-Latinos are appreciating more their Latino neighbor who lives just next door, and vice versa," said Stavans.

U.S. citizens of all backgrounds are picking up on the infectious *sabor latino* and becoming more integrated into the Latino culture, learning Spanish, taking salsa and Spanish guitar lessons, traveling to Latin America and becoming involved in local Hispanic events. More of them are intermarrying and creating bicultural families, as well.

Latin Americans, for their part, have been heavily influenced by U.S. culture for decades, but that influence is increasing with every year.

The media have done much to speed the shift. Latin American viewers are as excited about the opening of the latest Star Wars movie as are their U.S. counterparts. Latin American theaters carry U.S. releases in all the major cities, and mass media networks from the United States have been broadcasting movies, sitcoms, and news throughout Latin America for years. But now, with greater access to satellite TV, the penetration is deeper, to small villages that didn't know anything about CNN in the past. Expansion of the major U.S. media companies into the Latin American market is another important trend. Currently, about 70 percent of the news broadcast throughout

Latin America comes from U.S. sources.

The culture transfer is personal and physical, as well as electronic. Each year thousands of immigrants go back and forth, carrying their culture here and then returning home, forever changed by their new culture.

"That will make the closeness more emphatic," says Stavans. "There are parts of Mexico that when you walk around, you think you are in Miami. It's the same in Santo Domingo or San Juan. No immigrant group ever experienced this erasing of margins, this level of closeness, before."

For South Americans, the physical distance will still remain more of a barrier than for Mexicans and Caribbean islanders. But if current trends are any indication, the American Dream's siren song will continue to sound south of the equator. It will continue to lure them, by the tens of thousands every year, members of each group bringing their own traditions, their own foods, and their own special *sazón* to add to the cultural salad bowl that is North America.

 Text-Dependent Questions

1. What was the dropout rate of Hispanic high school students in 2000? What was the rate in 2013?
2. What are some ways that Hispanics have become more visible in the media in recent years?

 **Research Project**

Choose a famous American or Canadian of South American descent and write a short profile of that person.

Famous South Americans

ISABEL ALLENDE (**1942–**   ), a best-selling novelist, fled from her native Chile when her uncle, President Salvador Allende, was assassinated. She raised her children in Venezuela, where she wrote her internationally acclaimed *The House of the Spirits*. She has maintained a prolific writing career ever since. Allende moved to Marin County, California, the home of her second husband, in the 1980s.

LUIS APARICIO (**1934–**   ), one of major-league baseball's greatest shortstops of all time, is a native of Venezuela. He was inducted into the Baseball Hall of Fame in 1984.

LOURDES BAIRD (**1935–**   ), a former federal judge who served on the U.S. District Court for the Central District of California from 1992 until 2005. Baird went to law school after marrying and raising her three children. She was born in Ecuador and moved to the United States when she was one year old.

FERNANDO BOTERO (**1932–**   ) is a beloved painter and illustrator whose whimsical images feature chubby figures that hearken back to colonial times. His paintings are featured in the most important museums in Latin America, Europe, and the United States. He moved from his native Medellín, Colombia, to New York in 1960.

WILLIAM CHIGNOLI (**1938–**   ), a minister and psychologist, has led the efforts to help integrate new Latino immigrants in the St. Louis area. He is the founder of Acción Social Comunitaria (Social Action Group) and La Clínica, a clinic aimed at the uninsured Spanish-speaking population of the region. He is from Santa Fe, Argentina.

MANDALIT DEL BARCO (**1959–**   ) is a radio and print journalist specializing in Latino and Latin American issues. Del Barco reports for National Public Radio, Latino USA, and *Latina* magazine, and has been on the staffs of the *Miami Herald* and the *Village Voice*.

JAIME ESCALANTE (**1930–2010**), a brilliant teacher in the mostly Hispanic East Los Angeles Garfield High School, won acclaim for his success with at-risk teenagers. He was the subject of the popular 1988 movie *Stand and Deliver*. President Ronald Reagan called him a hero on national television. He was born in La Paz, Bolivia, and came to the United States in 1964 to escape the political unrest.

FRANCISCO GÓMEZ-DALLMEIER (1953–   ), a biodiversity and conservation biologist from Caracas, Venezuela, serves as the director of the Man and the Biosphere program for the Smithsonian Institution in Washington, D.C., and coordinates field biodiversity research and training throughout Latin America.

CAROLINA HERRERA (1939–   ) is a New York–based fashion designer from Caracas, Venezuela. Herrera's designs have clothed the rich and famous, including First Ladies Jacqueline Kennedy Onassis and Nancy Reagan. She has won numerous awards, including a spot in the Fashion Hall of Fame. She became a naturalized U.S. citizen in 2009.

MARIO KREUTZBERGER (1940–   ), best known as Don Francisco, is a popular personality on the Unavision network in the United States. He was the host of the variety programs *Sábado Gigante* and *Don Francisco Presenta*.

CARLOS NORIEGA (1959–   ), an astronaut, was born in Lima, Peru, but moved to California as a child and now considers Santa Clara his hometown. He has logged more than 461 hours in space, including a 1997 mission aboard the space shuttle *Atlantis*.

MAGGIE PEÑA (1959–   ), an entrepreneur and cofounder of the National Society of Hispanic MBAs, has worked hard to increase the number of Hispanic business students in graduate schools. She was born in Bogotá, Colombia, and moved to Los Angeles, California, when she was seven.

Series Glossary of Key Terms

assimilate—to adopt the ways of another culture; to fully become part of a different country or society.

census—an official count of a country's population.

deport—to forcibly remove someone from a country, usually back to his or her native land.

green card—a document that denotes lawful permanent resident status in the United States.

migrant laborer—an agricultural worker who travels from region to region, taking on short-term jobs.

naturalization—the act of granting a foreign-born person citizenship.

passport—a paper or book that identifies the holder as the citizen of a country; usually required for traveling to or through other foreign lands.

undocumented immigrant—a person who enters a country without official authorization; sometimes referred to as an "illegal immigrant."

visa—official authorization that permits arrival at a port of entry but does not guarantee admission into the United States.

Further Reading

Bourke, Dale Hanson. *Immigration: Tough Questions, Direct Answers.* Downers Grove, IL: InterVarsity Press, 2014.

Chomsky, Aviva. *Undocumented: How Immigration Became Illegal.* Boston: Beacon Press, 2014.

Gjelten, Tom. *A Nation of Nations: A Great American Immigration Story.* New York: Simon and Schuster, 2015.

Gonzalez, Juan. *Harvest of Empire: A History of Latinos in America.* New York: Viking Press, 2002.

Merino, Noel. *Illegal Immigration.* San Diego: Greenhaven Press, 2015.

Reyes, Angel, and Bradley Ewing. *Hispanic Immigration.* Lubbock, Texas: Mead Publishing, 2014.

Internet Resources

www.uscis.gov

The website of U.S. Citizenship and Immigration Services explains the various functions of the organization and provides specific information on immigration policy.

www.canadianhistory.ca/iv/main.html

This site contains an excellent history of immigration to Canada from the 1800s to the present.

www.cia.gov/library/publications/the-world-factbook

The CIA World Factbook includes links to demographic, political, economic, and historical information about all the countries of South America.

http://migration.ucdavis.edu

The website Migration News, run by the University of California-Davis, provides information on immigration issues, including a monthly summary of trends.

www.pewresearch.org

The Pew Research Center produces a wide range of research on Hispanic and immigration issues.

Index

Numbers in **bold italic** refer to captions.

Contributors

Senior consulting editor STUART ANDERSON is an adjunct scholar at the Cato Institute and executive director of the National Foundation for American Policy. From August 2001 to January 2003, he served as executive associate commissioner for Policy and Planning and Counselor to the Commissioner at the Immigration and Naturalization Service. He spent four and a half years on Capitol Hill on the Senate Immigration Subcommittee, first for Senator Spencer Abraham and then as Staff Director of the subcommittee for Senator Sam Brownback. Prior to that, Stuart was Director of Trade and Immigration Studies at the Cato Institute, where he produced reports on the military contributions of immigrants and the role of immigrants in high technology. Stuart has published articles in the Wall Street Journal, New York Times, Los Angeles Times, and other publications. He has an M.A. from Georgetown University and a B.A. in Political Science from Drew University. His articles have appeared in such publications as the *Wall Street Journal*, *New York Times*, and *Los Angeles Times*.

MARIAN L. SMITH served as the senior historian of the U.S. Immigration and Naturalization Service (INS) from 1988 to 2003, and is currently the immigration and naturalization historian within the Department of Homeland Security in Washington, D.C. She studies, publishes, and speaks on the history of the immigration agency and is active in the management of official 20th-century immigration records.

PETER HAMMERSCHMIDT is director general of national cyber security at Public Safety Canada. He previously served as First Secretary (Financial and Military Affairs) for the Permanent Mission of Canada to the United Nations. Before taking this position, he was a ministerial speechwriter and policy specialist for the Department of National Defence in Ottawa. Prior to joining the public service, he served as the Publications Director for the Canadian Institute of Strategic Studies in Toronto. He has a B.A. (Honours) in Political Studies from Queen's University, and an MScEcon in Strategic Studies from the University of Wales, Aberystwyth.

LARRY MCCAFFREY is a freelance writer and editor. He is a resident of Tampa, where he lives with his wife Esperanza and their five children. This is his first book.

Picture Credits